Grammar Sense

WORKBOOK 3

Angela Blackwell and Karen Davy

OXFORD

UNIVERSITY PRESS

OXFORD
UNIVERSITY PRESS

198 Madison Avenue
New York, NY 10016 USA

Great Clarendon Street
Oxford OX2 6DP England

Oxford   New York
Auckland   Bangkok   Buenos Aires   Cape Town   Chennai
Dar es Salaam   Delhi   Hong Kong   Istanbul   Karachi   Kolkata
Kuala Lumpur   Madrid   Melbourne   Mexico City   Mumbai
Nairobi   São Paulo   Shanghai   Taipei   Tokyo   Toronto

OXFORD is a trademark of Oxford University Press.

ISBN 0-19-436577-8

Copyright © 2003 Oxford University Press

Editorial Manager: Janet Aitchison
Editorial Development, Project Management,
  and Production: Marblehead House, Inc.
Production Manager: Shanta Persaud
Production Coordinator: Zainaltu Jawat Ali

Illustrations: Roger Penwill
Cover Design: Lee Ann Dollison
Cover Photo: Kevin Schafer / Peter Arnold, Inc.

The authors and publisher are grateful for permission to reprint the following photographs:

p. 7 ©Jon Feingersh / CORBIS; **p. 8** ©The Dian Fossey Gorilla Fund International
(www.gorillafund.org); **p. 13** ©Jack Hollingsworth / Photodisc ; **p. 22** ©Charlotte Casey; **p. 29** ©AFP /
CORBIS; **p. 34** ©CORBIS; **p. 59** ©Dennis Degnan / CORBIS; **p. 69** ©EyeWire / Getty Images; **p. 94**
©Bobby Model; **p. 96** ©George D. Lepp / CORBIS; **p.101** ©Mitchell Gerber / CORBIS; **p. 121**
©Rob Lewine / CORBIS

The authors and publisher are grateful for permission to reprint the following text excerpts:

p. 75: ©The Irish Times. Reprinted with permission; **p. 76**: from *More Random Acts of Kindness*.
Yorkville, ME: Conari Press, 1994; **p. 80**: ©2000 Newsday, Inc. Reprinted with permission; **p. 84**:
based on an excerpt from the San Francisco State University Extended Learning catalog: "Summer
Study in Paris." Reprinted with permission; **p. 85**: from "All About Allergies," ©Readers Digest (UK
Edition), July, 2000; **p. 87**: from "Life's Like That," ©Readers Digest (UK Edition), March, 2000;
p. 88: from "Variety of Vitamin-Rich Melons Is Slice of Summertime Life," ©2000 Dale Ann Ogar.
Reprinted with permission; **p. 94**: Reprinted with permission of The Associated Press; **p. 96**:
Reprinted with permission of The Associated Press; **p. 101**: ©Chuck Thompson. Reprinted with
permission; **p. 104**: from "All in a Day's Work," ©Readers Digest (UK Edition), July, 2000

Printing (last digit): 10 9 8 7 6 5 4 3 2 1

Printed in Hong Kong

Contents

CHAPTER

1 The Present

FORM

1 Examining Form

Read this newspaper article and complete the tasks below.

In Japan, *Kyoiku Mamas* Help Kids Succeed in School

TOKYO, Japan—Eleven-year-old Fumie is always tired. She is in the fifth grade. Three days a week, she <u>rushes</u> home from school, eats a 5 quick snack, and then runs out again on her way to *juku*, or cram school. She's preparing to enter a good private school next year.

Her three-and-a-half-year-old 10 brother, Koichi, goes to nursery school. He's getting ready to take one of the most important examinations of his life—entrance into the first grade.

15 These children are likely to do well because their mother knows what it takes to succeed in today's highly competitive Japan. She's called a *kyoiku mama*, or "education 20 mother." The education mother studies with her children, takes them to special classes, and hires tutors for them. She never leaves them in the hands of a babysitter 25 even if she does sometimes want to have an afternoon for herself. She knows that her children's time is too important for that. In contrast, Japanese fathers don't get as 30 involved in their children's education. They usually work very late and come home long after their families are already in bed.

Today more Japanese are 35 becoming aware of the harmful effects of too much studying. They realize that their children are spending too much time with their books, playing too little, and 40 possibly sleeping too little. But until the system changes, the *kyoiku mama* is unlikely to go away.

1. There are many examples of the simple present in the article. The first one is underlined. Underline eight more. (Don't include forms of *be*.)

2. There are six examples of the present continuous. The first one is circled. Circle five more.

3. Find the sentence in the simple present that includes *does* and draw a box around it. Why did the writer use *does*? Check the correct answer.

_____ **a.** The sentence is a question.

_____ **b.** The sentence is a statement that uses *does* for emphasis.

2 Asking Simple Present *Yes/No* and Information Questions

Read the answers below. Use the information in parentheses to write a simple present question for each answer.

1. (Koichi/go/to elementary school)

    Q: _Does Koichi go to elementary school?_

    A: No, he doesn't. He goes to nursery school.

2. (his sister Fumie/study/in sixth grade)

    Q: _____

    A: No she doesn't. She studies in fifth grade.

3. (how many days/she/go/to juku)

    Q: _____

    A: Three days a week.

4. (their mother/study/with her children)

    Q: _____

    A: Yes, she does.

5. (she/teach them/herself)

    Q: _____

    A: No, she doesn't. She hires tutors.

6. (why/Japanese fathers/not get involved/in their children's education)

    Q: _____

    A: Because they usually work very late.

7. (when/they/usually/come/home)

    Q: _____

    A: Long after their families are in bed asleep.

8. (what/more Japanese/realize/today)

    Q: _____

    A: Their children study too much and play too little.

Complete this paragraph with the present continuous form of the verbs in parentheses. Use contractions when possible.

 Reporter: This is Chris Meeks in Wimbledon, England, next to the courts on the first day of the tennis tournament. Right now the sun _is shining_ (shine), and the seats _____ (fill up) quickly. Today, here on center court, we _____ (look) forward to watching a thrilling opening match. Here come the players. They _____ (walk) onto the court. What _____ the American, Michael Powell, _____ (do)? _____ he _____ (argue) with the Australian, Tim Chang? No, I'm sorry. He _____ (not/argue) with him. I think he _____ just _____ (wish) him good luck. Well, the players _____ (take off) their warm-up suits and the game _____ finally _____ (get started). Powell _____ (take) a last drink of water, and Chang _____ (do) the same. The crowd _____ (make) a lot of noise, and the officials _____ (raise) their hands to ask them to quiet down. Here we go. Chang _____ (start) his serve . . .

MEANING AND USE

Read this conversation and complete the tasks below.

Ana: Hey, Carlos. How are you doing? How are things?

Carlos: Good. I'm back at college. I'm working on a degree in biology at Rutgers. It's a lot of work, but I love it.

Ana: Fantastic! That's a great school. And are you living near campus?

Carlos: I'm living at home with my parents—just for this semester.

Ana: How are you getting along with them?

Carlos: We get along OK, except they're always asking me where I'm going and when I'm coming home.

Ana: Well, you know what they say: "To your parents, you never grow up. You're always their child."

Carlos: Yeah, I guess that's right. But most of the time, things are fine. Especially because we hardly see each other. I leave for school every morning at 7:00 and don't get home until 11:00 at night.

Ana: So, will you be taking classes this summer?

Carlos: I don't think so. Every summer I work at my uncle's restaurant to help my family.

1. Read these sentences from the conversation. Write *SP* if they are in the simple present, and *PC* if they are in the present continuous.

   __PC__ **1.** I'm working on a degree in biology at Rutgers.

   _____ **2.** I'm living at home with my parents—just for this semester.

   _____ **3.** . . . except they're always asking me where I'm going and when I'm coming home.

   _____ **4.** "To your parents, you never grow up. You're always their child."

   _____ **5.** I leave for school every morning at 7:00, and I don't get home until 11:00 at night.

   _____ **6.** Every summer I work at my uncle's restaurant to help my family.

2. Now match each sentence to its use below.

   __5__ **a.** describing a routine   _____ **d.** making a complaint

   _____ **b.** expressing an activity in the   _____ **e.** describing a general truth
   extended present
   _____ **f.** describing a temporary
   _____ **c.** describing a habitual situation   situation

Understanding Verbs with Stative and Active Meanings

Read the sentences below. Write *S* for sentences that express states or conditions.
Write *A* for sentences that express actions.

___S___ **1.** I own a bicycle.

_____ **2.** I ride my bicycle after work.

_____ **3.** I love riding my bicycle.

_____ **4.** I also work out at a gym.

_____ **5.** I usually lift weights at the gym.

_____ **6.** I believe that exercise is important.

_____ **7.** I don't understand lazy people.

_____ **8.** I feel good after exercising.

COMBINING FORM, MEANING, AND USE

Thinking About Meaning and Use

Choose the correct response to each statement or question. There may be more than
one correct answer for each.

1. "I'm living in a small apartment on Center Street."

   The speaker . . .
   a. is complaining
   b. thinks her living situation is temporary
   c. is describing an action in progress
   d. wants to stay where she is

2. "What does Yuko do?"

   The speaker wants to know . . .
   a. Yuko's daily schedule
   b. Yuko's occupation
   c. a general truth about Yuko
   d. the way Yuko feels

3. "I don't sleep more than four or five hours a night."

   The speaker is talking about a . . .
   a. routine
   b. physical sensation
   c. general truth
   d. definition

4. "I really love this computer game."

   The speaker is . . .
   a. not playing the game
   b. expressing an emotion
   c. describing a typical quality
   d. expressing a physical sensation

5. "Fewer and fewer planes are flying to Italy this summer."

   The speaker is describing a . . .
   a. routine
   b. permanent situation
   c. changing situation
   d. habitual situation

6. "How often do you go to the doctor?"

   The speaker is asking about . . .
   a. an action in progress
   b. a general truth
   c. a person's routine
   d. a changing situation

7. "Beef contains more fat than poultry or fish."

   The speaker is talking about . . .
   a. a physical sensation
   b. a general truth
   c. a changing situation
   d. an emotion

8. "Police are questioning more than a dozen people about the crime."

   The speaker is describing . . .
   a. an action in progress
   b. a habitual situation
   c. a typical quality
   d. a changing situation

There are eleven errors in this magazine advice column. The first one has been corrected. Find and correct ten more.

Ask Dr. Frank

Dear Dr. Frank:

I ~~write~~ 'm writing this letter because I have a serious problem. I work in a stressful job, but I'm not believing it's worse than what most people face at work. My problem is that I'm crying too easily when things goes wrong. I knowing I have to get stronger. I don't deal well with disappointment or criticism. It's being very embarrassing. In fact, the situation becomes more and more difficult. What advice do you have for me?

Cry Baby in Dallas

Dear Cry Baby:

Most of us gets upset when others criticize us. But you are being right: You're not appearing professional when you cry at work. Sometimes we needs to cry, but tears don't belongs on the job. If you think you're going to cry, go to the restroom and do it there. And please, see a therapist to help you with your emotions.

Arlene Frank, M.D.

Follow the steps below to write a descriptive paragraph.

1. Find a photograph or drawing that shows a lot of activity. Study the picture carefully. What activities are happening? List some of the activities that you see. Then write notes describing people or objects in the picture.

2. On a separate sheet of paper, use your notes to write a detailed paragraph describing your picture. Use the present continuous to tell what is happening in the picture. Use the simple present to describe the people and objects.

> Here's a picture of my family at a picnic. My father is getting the fire ready for the barbecue. He's the large man in shorts . . . .

2 The Past

FORM

 Examining Form

Read this short biography and complete the tasks below.

The Lonely Woman of the Forest

Dian Fossey and friend

American zoologist Dian Fossey first (became) interested in Africa in the early 1960s. She traveled there in 1963 and met the famous anthropologist Louis Leakey. Once, while Fossey and Leakey were talking 5 about mountain gorillas, she expressed her wish to study these animals' behavior. Four years later, she returned to Africa with a research grant from the National Geographic Society.

The mountain gorilla was becoming extinct when Fossey began her research. 10 Soon, she was at war with poachers who were killing gorillas in Rwanda's Parc National des Volcans. She also opposed Rwandan authorities, who hoped to open the park to tourism. In fact, she threatened to shoot any tourist who approached her station.

This dedication to her gorilla friends earned her enemies. One night in 1985, 15 Fossey was killed while she was sleeping at her campsite in the mountains of Rwanda.

Fossey's work made her a legend. At one time, there were only ten gorilla families still alive. Today, that number has more than doubled–thanks to "the lonely woman of the forest."

becoming extinct: dying out   **poacher:** a person who kills animals illegally

grant: money that is awarded for a specific purpose

1. There are many examples of the simple past in the biography. The first one is circled. Circle eight more. (Don't include forms of *be*.)

2. There are four examples of the past continuous. The first one is underlined. Underline three more.

3. There are three examples of time clauses beginning with *while* and *when*. One has a box around it. Find two more.

Use the cues to write conversations. Write *Conversation 1* in the simple past and *Conversation 2* in the past continuous.

Conversation 1

Rosa: why/be/you/late again this morning?

   Why were you late again this morning?

Hector: I/oversleep. I/not/wake up/until 8:30.

_____

Rosa: your boss/see/you?

_____

Hector: she/see/me/when/I/come/in.

_____

Rosa: she/say/anything to you?

_____

Hector: she/not/say/anything, but she/give/me a dirty look.

_____

Conversation 2

Elena: you and Sasha/make/a lot of noise last night.

   You and Sasha were making a lot of noise last night.

Eva: sorry. you/try/to sleep?

_____

Elena: no. I/not/sleep. I/read.

_____

Eva: well, first Sasha and I/watch/a great TV program.

_____

Elena: is that why/you/laugh/so hard?

_____

Eva: for part of the time. Later, we/laugh/because we/look at/some old pictures of you!

_____

MEANING AND USE

A. Complete these questions with the most logical simple past ending from the choices in the *Time Clauses* box below.

```
┌─────────────────────────────────────────────┐
│              TIME CLAUSES                     │
│                                               │
│   before you had a car                        │
│                                               │
│   when you lived in the Caribbean             │
│                                               │
│   when you were growing up                    │
│                                               │
│   while you were at college                   │
│                                               │
│   when you ate in that fancy restaurant       │
│                                               │
│   after I gave you my number                  │
└─────────────────────────────────────────────┘
```

1. How was the weather _when you lived in the Caribbean?_

2. What did you order _____

3. Why didn't you call me _____

4. What did you and your family do together at night _____

5. How did you get around _____

6. How did you pay your tuition _____

B. Look at the questions in part A. Match the questions with these responses.

____4____ **a.** We played games, talked, and watched TV.

_____ **b.** Sorry. I meant to, but I got busy.

_____ **c.** I had a seafood salad.

_____ **d.** I always borrowed money from my parents.

_____ **e.** It used to rain every afternoon.

_____ **f.** I usually took the bus.

C. Look again at the questions in part A. Which questions are asking about:

a. __1_____ actions or states that lasted a long period of time?

b. _____ actions that lasted a short period of time?

4 Contrasting the Simple Past and the Past Continuous

Complete this story with the simple past or past continuous forms of the verbs in parentheses. Use contractions when possible.

I <u>ran into</u> (run into) an old friend yesterday. My wife and I
_____ (wait for) the light to change when I _____ (hear)
someone call my name. I _____ (look) around, but I _____
(not see) anyone that I _____ (know). Finally, I _____ (see) Jake.
He _____ (stand) on a platform high in the air, and he _____
(wash) the windows of a very tall building. "I'll be right down," he _____
(call). A few minutes later, I _____ (shake) Jake's hand and
_____ (introduce) him to my wife. We _____ (chat) for a few
minutes, but while we _____ (talk), I _____ (realize) how late it
_____ (get). So my wife and I _____ (say) good-bye to Jake.

5 Using the Simple Past and the Past Continuous in Time Clauses

A. Choose the correct clause to complete each sentence.

1. _____ , I always dreamt of working at the United Nations.
   a. When I grew up
   b. When I was growing up

2. When the fire alarm sounded, _____ .
   a. we were taking an important exam
   b. we took an important exam

3. The motorcycle came to a sudden stop _____ .
   a. after the driver saw a stop sign
   b. while the driver was seeing a stop sign

4. _____ , we all jumped.
   a. When the balloon was popping
   b. When the balloon popped

5. When the forest fire began near our town, _____ .
   a. almost everyone went to sleep
   b. most of the town was sleeping

6. _____ when I heard the noise.
   a. I was getting scared
   b. I got scared

B. Match each sentence in part A to its meaning below. Some of the sentences have more than one correct answer.

1. <u>d</u>   a. cause and effect

2. _____   b. sequential events

3. _____   c. an interrupted event

4. _____   d. action in progress over an extended period of time

5. _____   e. action in progress at an exact moment

6. _____

COMBINING FORM, MEANING, AND USE

Read each situation. Then choose the sentences that are true. Some of the situations have more than one correct answer.

1. He cut his foot before he mowed the lawn.

   a. After he cut his foot, he mowed the lawn.

   b. He cut his foot while he was mowing the lawn.

   c. First, he cut his foot. Then he moved the lawn.

2. I was shopping when I remembered my friend's birthday.

   a. I was shopping because it was my friend's birthday.

   b. I didn't remember my friend's birthday until I went shopping.

   c. While I was shopping, I realized it was my friend's birthday.

3. We were having a meeting when the boss arrived.

   a. First, the meeting started. Then the boss arrived.

   b. The meeting started before the boss arrived.

   c. The boss arrived. Then the meeting started.

4. Before she met Peter, she was dating a nice Spanish man.

   a. First, she went out with Peter. Then she met a Spanish man.

   b. She was seeing Peter when she met a Spanish man.

   c. She went out with a Spanish man before she met Peter.

5. The phone was ringing when I got to the door.

   a. I opened the door before the phone rang.

   b. The phone started ringing before I opened the door.

   c. After I opened the door, the phone started ringing.

6. When they built the new library, we didn't have to go downtown anymore.

   a. We went downtown before they built the new library.

   b. We didn't have to go downtown while they were building the new library.

   c. We didn't have to go downtown after they built the new library.

There are fourteen errors in this student's composition. The first one has been corrected. Find and correct thirteen more.

I have
~~I'm having~~ so many wonderful memories of my childhood. While I was three years old, my family moved to Costa Rica. For the first few years, we lived in a small apartment. Then, when it's time for my brother and me to start school, my parents were buying our first house. For the first time, I had my own room and didn't had to share with my sister. I was loving that room! My mother was liking to sew, and she made a beautiful bedspread and matching curtains.

We didn't have a lot of free time during the week, but weekends were always being a lot of fun. On Saturdays, we always play games together. Sunday was my favorite day because we almost always went to the beach. We were packing a big lunch, and Dad barbecue hamburgers or chicken. We kids were being sleepy after we were eating, so we spread blankets under a big tree and take naps.

On a separate sheet of paper, write a two-paragraph essay about a time when you first heard about an important event. Use the simple past and the past continuous when possible.

1. First, list some important world or family news to write about in your paragraphs.

   In the first paragraph, say what the event was and write about your situation when you heard the news. Where were you and what were you doing? Were you working, playing, studying? Were you alone or were you with other people?

2. In the second paragraph, write about your reactions to the news. What did you feel and think? Do you remember what you did later that day? How did the event affect your own life after that?

>   I remember the night when the Anaheim Angels won the World Series. I was sitting in my room at my desk. I was studying for an important exam. My brother came in and told me . . . .

3 Future Forms

FORM

Read these interviews and complete the tasks below.

Lisa Rodriguez
Woman About Town

Views of the Future

Today our "Woman About Town" reporter, Lisa Rodriguez, asked people on the street this question: What <u>will</u> things <u>be</u> like thirty years from now?

"The science magazines say
5 that there are going to be a lot
of medical breakthroughs.
For example, researchers will
be growing body parts, such
as hearts, livers, and hands in
10 labs and transplanting them
into people."—**Sam Leonard,
56, stockbroker**

"Because of global warming,
the climate will get a lot
15 warmer. People won't be
traveling to places like Hawaii
anymore to get away from the
cold." –**Marta Michaels, 37,
hairdresser**

20 "The transportation system
will be really different. For
example, the taxis. Instead of
cars driving on the streets,
they'll be flying in the air. If
25 you want to go to the airport,
a flying taxi will come and
pick you up at your house."
–**Jorge Sanchez, 24,
postal worker**

30 "I think people and animals
will understand each other
better. Someone will invent a
new kind of language, and
people and animals will talk
35 with each other. That's
possible, don't you think?"
–**Andrea Smith, 13, student**

"Maybe I'm a pessimist, but
I think there's a fifty/fifty
40 chance that there will be a
big catastrophe. I think there
will be a big earthquake.
When that happens, a lot of
people will die." –**Robert
45 Grasso, 68, retired**

"What will things be like in
the future? I hope much
better, but how do I know?
My restaurant is going out of
50 business next week, and I
need to find another job. I
can't think about what I'll be
doing thirty years from now."
–**Barbara Chu, 35, waitress**

---

1. There are many examples of future forms in the interviews. The first one is underlined. Underline eight more.

2. Find a future time clause with *when* and circle it.

3. Check the correct statement about future time clauses.

_____ **a.** We use the simple present in the main clause and a different future form in the time clause.

_____ **b.** We use *will*, *be going to*, or a future continuous form in the main clause and the simple present in the time clause.

_____ **c.** A time clause always comes before the main clause.

Read the reasons Ben's friends can't come to his party on Saturday. Write sentences in the future continuous about what they will be doing instead.

1. **Ana and Miguel:** "We have tickets to a play downtown."

   Ana and Miguel will be watching a play downtown.

2. **Jane:** "I promised to teach my nieces how to bowl."

   _____

3. **David:** "I told my grandmother I'd go shopping with her."

   _____

4. **Takeshi:** "I have to help Jessica."

   _____

5. **Celia:** "I absolutely must catch up on my homework."

   _____

6. **Rachel:** "You won't believe it. I have to work!"

   _____

3 **Working on the Simple Present as Future**

Look at the Independence Day Celebration poster. Then complete the conversation, using the simple present as future and the verbs *begin, cost, end, last,* and *start.*

Eric: When does the celebration begin?
₁

Bill: _____ on Friday at noon.
₂

Eric: _____
₃

Bill: _____ on Sunday night, after
₄
the fireworks.

Eric: _____
₅

Bill: _____ on Saturday morning.
₆
They're going to be exciting this year.

Eric: _____
₇

Bill: _____ all day Saturday and
₈
half the day on Sunday.

Eric: _____
₉

Bill: _____ $5.00 a day for adults
₁₀
and $2.50 for kids.

> ## Chatham Independence Day Celebration
>
> **SCHEDULE OF EVENTS**
> **Friday**
> • Opening festivities
>   Noon to midnight
> **Saturday**
> • Boat races
>   8:00 a.m.–6:00 p.m.
> **Sunday**
> • Boat Races
>   9:00 a.m.–noon
> • Giant barbecue and picnic
>   Noon–4:00 p.m.
> • Jazz Concert
>   6:00 p.m.–8:30 p.m.
> • Fireworks
>   9:00 p.m.–10:00 p.m.
>
> | Tickets: $5.00/day for adults |
> | $2.50/day for children |

MEANING AND USE

4 **Contrasting Future Forms**

Choose one, two, or three correct phrases to complete each sentence.

1. It looks like ____ in a little while.
   - **a.** it clears up
   - **b.** it's going to clear up *(circled)*
   - **c.** it's clearing up

2. ____ a party next Saturday?
   - **a.** Do you have
   - **b.** Are you going to have
   - **c.** Are you having

3. I feel lucky. I think ____ the lottery this week.
   - **a.** I'm winning
   - **b.** I'm going to win
   - **c.** I win

4. The meeting ____ at 2:30 on Friday.
   - **a.** starts
   - **b.** is starting
   - **c.** is going to start

5. In the year 2025, our refrigerators ____ their own food.
   - **a.** will order
   - **b.** order
   - **c.** are ordering

6. ____ into my new apartment on Saturday.
   - **a.** I'm moving
   - **b.** I move
   - **c.** I'm going to move

5 **Ordering Events with Future Time Clauses**

Lisa has invited some friends over for dinner. Look at her TO DO list. Use the time word(s) in parentheses to write the order of things she's going to do before her guests arrive. Use *going to* in the main clause.

1. (when) When she finishes work at the office, she's going to come home.

2. (before) _____

3. (after) _____

4. (as soon as) _____

5. (until) _____

6. (after) _____

> **TO DO**
>
> 1. Come home. Finish work at the office.
>
> 2. Write down the grocery list. Go food shopping.
>
> 3. Take it out of the oven. Bake the turkey for 6 hours at 375°.
>
> 4. Polish the silver. Set the table.
>
> 5. Prepare all ingredients for the salad. Wait to add the dressing.
>
> 6. Wash the kitchen floor. Sweep the kitchen floor.

COMBINING FORM, MEANING, AND USE

6 **Thinking About Meaning and Use**

Use each set of cues to write two conversations. Use the present continuous as future and the future with *going to* in each conversation.

1. **Hiro:** What/you/do/next Saturday?

    Koji: Yuko and I/spend/the day at the beach.

    a. Hiro: What are you doing next Saturday?

    Koji: Yuko and I are going to spend the day at the beach.

    b. Hiro: _____

    Koji: _____

2. **Ben:** When/you/finish/final exams?

    Kevin: I/finish/next week.

    a. Ben: _____

    Kevin: _____

    b. Ben: _____

    Kevin: _____

3. **David:** How/you/celebrate/your birthday this year?

    Kate: My parents/throw/me/a big party.

    a. David: _____

    Kate: _____

    b. David: _____

    Kate: _____

4. **Emily:** What/you/do/after graduation?

    Tony: I/leave/on a trip to Mexico.

    a. Emily: _____

    Tony: _____

    b. Emily: _____

    Tony: _____

There are nine errors in these paragraphs. The first one has been corrected. Find and correct eight more.

> _will have_
> People predict that genetic engineering ~~has~~ a major effect on our food supply in the future. Genetically engineered fruits, vegetables, and animals will help increase the food supply. For example, it is possible that people are growing tropical fruits such as bananas, coconuts, and pineapples in colder climates such as Canada or Russia. Foods on supermarket shelves are going taste better and last longer. Since these foods won't spoil as quickly, they are being abundant and cheap.
>
> These new foods also going to be better for you. Scientists manipulate the DNA of many foods to make them more nutritious and allergy-free. Potatoes will be having a special gene so that when people make French fries, they aren't soaking up as much oil. And there may even be special fruits and vegetables that act like vaccines. So instead of getting a shot to prevent disease, people are eating an apple or a carrot!

On a separate sheet of paper, write a paragraph about your vision of the future. Use the future with _will_ and _going to_, the present continuous and the simple present as future, the future continuous, and future time clauses when possible.

Choose a time frame (such as 20 years from now) and answer these questions:

1. Will the world be a better place than it is now? Why or why not?

2. What kind of social changes will there be? What kind of work will people do? How will people spend their free time? How will they travel?

3. What will the environmental situation be like? Is there going to be more or less pollution? Will more animals be extinct?

> I think the world is probably going to be a better place in thirty years. There will be less poverty, and most people around the world will have enough to eat. At the same time, there will be more pollution . . . .

Chapters 1–3

A. Choose the correct clause to complete each sentence.

1. When I get home tonight, _____.
   a. I take a shower
   b. I took a shower
   c. I'm going to take a shower

2. Every day before she goes to work, _____.
   a. Barbara is feeding her cat
   b. Barbara feeds her cat
   c. Barbara was feeding her cat

3. I'm studying this semester, but _____.
   a. next year I look for a job
   b. next year I looked for a job
   c. next year I'll look for a job

4. Why didn't you take your umbrella _____?
   a. when it started to rain
   b. when it's starting to rain
   c. when it starts to rain

5. _____, my brother worked on his math assignment.
   a. While I was playing video games
   b. While I am playing video games
   c. While I play video games

6. As soon as I get my next paycheck, _____.
   a. I bought some new clothes
   b. I was buying some new clothes
   c. I'm going to buy some new clothes

7. Until _____, we can't take a trip.
   a. we save more money
   b. we'll save more money
   c. we saved more money

8. Today it's cloudy, and _____.
   a. the wind blows
   b. the wind is blowing
   c. the wind blew

9. I'll go home after _____.
   a. the game is going to be over
   b. the game is over
   c. the game will be over

10. _____ when I heard a loud noise.
    a. I will walk in the garden
    b. I walk in the garden
    c. I was walking in the garden

11. _____, please turn out the light.
    a. Before you are leaving the room
    b. Before you will leave the room
    c. Before you leave the room

12. _____ after you graduate from high school?
    a. What do you do
    b. What will you do
    c. What were you doing

13. _____ until you get back.
    a. I stay here
    b. I was staying here
    c. I'll stay here

14. Bill weighs too much, so _____.
    a. he decided to go on a diet
    b. he decides to go on a diet
    c. he decided to stop his diet

B. Find and correct the error in form, meaning, or use in each of these sentences.

15. How was the fire starting?

16. The children played in the yard when it started to rain.

17. The movie is about a group of teenagers who are getting lost in the forest.

18. I know these jeans are looking terrible, but all my other pants are in the laundry.

19. When Kedra was a child, she would have a lot of friends.

20. Marcus and I won't be getting marry next year because we just broke off our engagement.

21. The Chiefs will be the champions this year because they're definitely winning tomorrow night's game.

22. I promise that I will be finishing my homework.

23. If you have time, will you be stopping and pick up some bread on your way home?

24. Carlos is usually being very level-headed, but today he's overreacting to everything.

25. I was jogging in the park while I fell and hurt my left ankle.

C. Choose two **words or phrases to complete each sentence.**

26. Serena _____ a better player as she gets older.
    a. became   c. is becoming
    b. will become   d. becomes

27. When we were kids, we _____ understand the importance of getting enough sleep.
    a. don't   c. didn't
    b. couldn't   d. wouldn't

28. My tooth _____, so I think I will see a dentist.
    a. hurts   c. hurt
    b. is hurting   d. was hurting

29. What _____ when you saw the president?
    a. you did   c. did you
    b. were you doing d. did you do

30. We're happy they _____ a new supermarket on the corner.
    a. 're opening   c. open
    b. 'll open   d. opened

The Present Perfect

FORM

1 Examining Form

Read this article and complete the tasks below.

Finding a Way off the Streets

"If This Street Were Mine" performers

Alex Paga didn't plan to join the circus when he ran away from home at age eight. But he did—and it probably saved his life.

5 "If This Street Were Mine" is a program that uses circus arts to give the runaway and homeless children of Rio de Janeiro, Brazil, a second chance at life. Paga <u>has been</u> with the 10 program for over ten years, and he's now an acrobatics instructor.

Some 1,300 street children have gone through the program since it began in 1992, says its director, Cesar 15 Marques. Of the approximately 1,000 children the program has maintained contact with, only 200 have returned to the streets. Every year the program sends six children to the National 20 Circus School in Rio, and graduates have performed in countries from Argentina to Germany.

But Marques says the program isn't about turning children into clowns. It has succeeded at getting so many kids off the streets by building confidence and a 25 sense of responsibility. It seems that putting on shows teaches children to set goals and to accept tasks. In fact, some graduates of "If This Street Were Mine" who didn't make it as acrobats or clowns have found careers as mechanics or bricklayers. And that is something to smile about.

There are seven examples of verbs in the present perfect in the article. The first one is underlined. Underline six more.

Complete this conversation with the words in parentheses and the present perfect.
Use contractions when possible.

Kate: Where _have you been_ (you/be)?
1

Andre: Sorry we're late. We _____ (be) stuck in traffic for the past hour.
2

Kate: The traffic _____ (be) really awful lately, hasn't it?
3

Irina: You can say that again! So _____ (you/order) anything yet?
4

Kate: The waiter _____ (come) to the table several times since I got
5

here, but I _____ (not/order) anything because I wanted to wait
6

for you guys.

Irina: Well, I _____ (not/eat) all day, so I'm starving.
7

_____ (you/see) that waiter recently?
8

Kate: Yes. Here he comes now. Andre, you _____ (eat) here before.
9

What's good?

Andre: This is a great restaurant. I _____ (never/have) a bad meal here.
10

Everything's delicious.

Irina: It's a little expensive, though. We _____ (pay) at least fifteen
11

dollars for an entrée every time we _____ (have) dinner here.
12

Kate: Wow, you're right. Here's a pasta dish for eighteen dollars.

Irina: Hmm. They _____ (raise) the prices again. Look, Andre. That tuna
13

dish is twenty-five dollars now.

Waiter: Good evening. Well, I see you're all here now. _____ (you/decide)
14

what you'd like to order?

Andre: Uh . . . well, no, we haven't. I think we need a little more time.

Waiter: No problem. _____ (you/hear) about our specials tonight? They're
15

all very good! And we _____ (add) a new specialty to the menu—
16

chicken with a delicious mushroom sauce!

Irina: That sounds good. . . but how much does it cost?

MEANING AND USE

Read the information and complete the tasks below.

> ## Many Admit to Bending the Rules
> This poll shows the percentage of Americans who admit to doing the following at least once in their lives.
> - Driving faster than the speed limit ·············· 92%
> - Telling a white lie ·· 89%
> - Calling in sick to work when they were healthy ·········· 67%
> - Parking illegally ·· 60%
> - Cheating on an exam ······································57%
> - Writing a personal e-mail at work ·····················43%
> - Making a long-distance phone call at work ···········38%
> - Cutting into a line·· 19%

A. Write eight statements about what Americans admit to doing at least once in their lives. Be sure to write out the percentages.

1. _Ninety-two percent have driven faster than the speed limit._

2. _____

3. _____

4. _____

5. _____

6. _____

7. _____

8. _____

B. Look at the poll again. What questions were asked in the poll? Write the questions. Then write your own answers.

1. Q: _Have you ever driven faster than the speed limit?_

   A: _Yes, I have. I've driven faster than the speed limit many times._

   OR   No, I haven't. I've never driven faster than the speed limit.

2. Q: _____

   A: _____

3. Q: _____

   A: _____

4. Q: _____

    A: _____

5. Q: _____

    A: _____

6. Q: _____

    A: _____

7. Q: _____

    A: _____

8. Q: _____

    A: _____

4   **Writing About Recent Past Time and Continuing Time up to Now**

Complete this story with *lately, recently, just, for,* and *since.* In some sentences, more than one answer is possible.

I've lived in the same house all my life. The Rosses have been our next-door

neighbors _for_ almost ten years now. Amy Ross and I have been best
       1

friends _____ we were in junior high school. Amy and I used to be
      2

inseparable, but I haven't seen much of her _____ . Amy and her boyfriend,
           3

Matt, have been very busy _____ . You see, Amy and Matt have
         4

_____ announced their engagement. They decided that they wanted to get
   5

married a few months ago, but they didn't tell anyone but me. I've kept their secret

_____ almost three months, and I'm very glad I don't have to keep the secret
   6

anymore. They've known each other _____ their first year in college, and
         7

they've been in love _____ five years. I miss my friend a lot these days, but
      8

I'm really happy for her. I know that she and Matt will be very happy.

Gina and Steve are going to Argentina. They've made lists of things to do. Now they're asking each other about what they've done. Use the information in the lists and the cues in parentheses to write questions and responses.

```
Gina's "to do" list

✔ Renew passports
  Pick up tickets at travel agency
  Reserve a rental car
✔ Shop for summer clothes
  Get film and toiletries
  Type up itinerary
```

```
Steve's "to do" list

✔ Make plane reservations
✔ Choose a hotel in Buenos Aires
  Pay the room deposit
✔ Buy travel insurance
✔ Shop for summer clothes
```

1. **Gina:** (make the plane reservations)

   Have you made the plane reservations yet?

   Steve: (yesterday)

   Yes, I have. I made them yesterday.

2. **Gina:** (choose a hotel in Buenos Aires)

   _____

   Steve: (the Olympic)

   _____

3. **Gina:** (pay the room deposit)

   _____

   Steve: (tomorrow)

   _____

4. **Steve:** (renew the passports)

   _____

   Gina: (on Wednesday)

   _____

5. **Steve:** (reserve a rental car)

   _____

   Gina: (too busy)

   _____

COMBINING FORM, MEANING, AND USE

Choose the correct ending for each sentence.

1. He does his job very well because
    a. he did it all his life.
    (b.) he's done it all his life.

2. We lived in Seattle for a few years,
    a. but we don't like it very much.
    b. but we didn't like it very much.

3. Hiro and Keiko were married for many years,
    a. and they had a very happy life together.
    b. and they've had a very happy life together.

4. I've washed these pants a million times,
    a. but they still look new.
    b. and they looked terrible.

5. I think the teacher is wrong. George Eliot, the nineteenth-century author,
    a. wrote more than three novels.
    b. has written more than three novels.

6. Some people think he was an excellent leader,
    a. but he's made a lot of mistakes during his presidency.
    b. but he made a lot of mistakes during his presidency.

7. The United States has never won the World Cup in soccer,
    a. but the team is improving in recent years.
    b. but the team has improved in recent years.

8. The headquarters of the United Nations has always been located in New York City,
    a. and most people think it's a good location for it.
    b. but most people thought it was a good location for it.

9. Last summer was the hottest one on record,
    a. but this summer has been even hotter.
    b. but we have had hotter summers.

10. Security in European airports has been strict for many years,
    a. and now it's become strict in the U.S.
    b. and now it became strict in the U.S.

On a separate sheet of paper, write two paragraphs about your travel experiences. Use present perfect and past forms when possible.

1. In the first paragraph, write about how much you have traveled in general. Answer these questions:

   • Have you traveled a lot?

   • What countries have you visited?

2. In the second paragraph, write about a place that you have visited more than once. Answer these questions:

   • How many times have you been there?

   • Have you always enjoyed going there?

   • What kinds of experiences have you had?

> I didn't travel much when I was a child, but since then I have traveled a lot. I have made several trips outside the country in the last five years . . . .

5 The Present Perfect Continuous

FORM

Read this magazine article and complete the tasks below.

What's Next for Steven Spielberg?

Moviegoers around the world have been looking forward to filmmaker Steven Spielberg's next film. What has he been working on these days? He hasn't discussed the details of his latest project, but judging 5 from the popularity and box-office success of his last several movies, he's been working with his usual creativity and passion.

Steven Spielberg

Steven Spielberg has been making films almost all his life. Born in 1947 in Cincinnati, Ohio, Spielberg 10 made his first film—thanks to his father's 8mm camera—when he was only 12. In 1970, he attracted attention with a short film that he made around the time he graduated from California State University, Long Beach. He became one of the youngest television directors at Universal Studios, and he was soon making 15 theatrically released motion pictures. His second film, *Jaws*, the thriller about a great white shark, has been frightening audiences since 1975. The string of hits that followed *Jaws*—including *E.T. the Extra-Terrestrial* (1982), the Academy Award-winning *Schindler's List* (1993), *Saving Private Ryan* (1998), and *Minority Report* (2002)—has made Steven Spielberg the most commercially successful director of 20 all time.

1. There are five examples of the present perfect continuous in the article. The first one is underlined. Underline four more.

2. Circle the main verb and draw a box around the two auxiliaries in the five examples. The first one is done for you.

Complete these conversations with the words in parentheses and the present perfect continuous. Use contractions when possible.

Conversation 1

Mother: Jenny, You've been on the phone all morning.

Who _have you been talking_ (you/talk) to?
₁

Daughter: I _____ (call) all my friends to tell them the good news about
₂

my scholarship.

Mother: Well, I hope no one _____ (try) to get through to me.
₃

I _____ (ask) you to get off the phone since 10:00. I'm
₄

expecting an important call.

Conversation 2

Ben: We haven't seen much of Kate lately. _____ (she/avoid) us?
₁

Teresa: Of course not. It's just that she _____ (work) overtime a lot.
₂

She _____ (get) home really late, so she _____
₃   ₄

(not/do) much besides work and sleep.

Ben: I hope she _____ (take care) of herself so she doesn't ruin
₅

her health.

Conversation 3

Interviewer: So the Olympics start tomorrow. How long _____
₁

(you/plan) for this event?

Sarah: I _____ (prepare) for the Olympics my entire life, and my
₂

parents _____ (make) sacrifices for years to help give me this
₃

opportunity.

Interviewer: And we _____ (watch) you for years. You _____
₄   ₅

(improve) your form and speed over the years, and you

_____ (skate) beautifully lately. The gold medal has your
₆

name on it!

Sarah: I hope you're right.

MEANING AND USE

Write sentences in the present perfect continuous about the situations below. Use *just, recently,* and *lately* when possible and join sentences with *and* or *because.* Use the phrases in the box.

> go to parties/study enough
>
> sleep well/have nightmares
>
> eat too much/exercise enough
>
> go straight home after work/go to the hospital to visit her uncle
>
> not spend time with friends/paint their house
>
> talk to his grandmother/not feel well

1. Julie used to be very fit, but she's gained a lot of weight.

   <u>She's been eating too much lately, and she hasn't been</u>

   <u>exercising enough.</u>

2. Paulo has always been a good student, but suddenly he isn't doing well in school.

   _____

   _____

3. Rick looks worried.

   _____

   _____

4. Kim has trouble staying awake at work.

   _____

   _____

5. The Normans usually have guests during the weekend, but they haven't had company for over a month.

   _____

   _____

6. Rita has been getting home from work later than usual.

   _____

   _____

4) Contrasting the Present Perfect Continuous and the Present Perfect

Choose the correct sentence to complete the conversations.

1. **Nancy:** That's a new skirt you're wearing, isn't it?

   Emily: _____
   a. This? I wore it for years.
   (b.) This? I've been wearing it for years.

2. **Paulo:** _____

   Pedro: I finished it last night.
   a. Have you finished the book yet?
   b. Have you returned the book?

3. **Alex:** _____

   Luisa: Yes, I have.
   a. Have you ever traveled to Italy?
   b. Did you go to Italy?

4. **Lee:** Do you see Chris a lot?

   Matt: _____
   a. Yes, I've seen him twice this week.
   b. Yes, I've met him.

5. **Carlos:** _____

   Hector: About twenty minutes.
   a. How long have you waited for me?
   b. How long have you been waiting for me?

6. **Irina:** At last! Some sunshine!

   Andre: I know. _____
   a. It's been raining all day.
   b. It just started to rain.

7. **Mrs. Ruiz:** _____

   Mr. Ruiz: Aren't they finished yet?
   a. The Carters have redecorated their apartment.
   b. The Carters have been redecorating their apartment.

8. **Satomi:** So what are we going to do?

   Tomiko: I'm not sure. _____
   a. I haven't decided.
   b. I haven't been deciding.

5) Contrasting the Present Perfect Continuous with Other Verb Forms

Complete these conversations with the words in parentheses and the present perfect continuous, the present perfect, or the simple past. In some sentences, more than one form is acceptable. Use contractions when possible.

Conversation 1

Celia: <u>Have you heard</u> (you/hear) from Kevin lately? I _____ (think) about
       $\quad\quad\quad\quad\quad$ 1 $\quad\quad\quad\quad\quad\quad\quad\quad\quad\quad\quad\quad$ 2
       him a lot recently.

Luisa: I _____ (not/speak) to him for ages, but he _____ (call)
       $\quad\quad\quad$ 3 $\quad\quad\quad\quad\quad\quad\quad\quad\quad\quad\quad\quad\quad$ 4
       Diane last week. Apparently, he _____ (travel) in Asia for business,
       $\quad\quad\quad\quad\quad\quad\quad\quad\quad\quad\quad\quad$ 5
       but he'll be back on Saturday. Diane _____ (promise) to pick him up
       $\quad\quad\quad\quad\quad\quad\quad\quad\quad\quad\quad\quad\quad\quad\quad$ 6
       at the airport.

Conversation 2

Keiko: _____ (you/read) this article?

₁

Yuko: No, I _____ (not/see) that magazine yet.

₂

Keiko: Well, it says here that Winona Ryder _____ (make) films since she was

₃
12 years old.

Yuko: Yes, I _____ (know) that. She _____ (work) in films for

₄ ₅
over half her life. But you know, I _____ (not/see) her in a movie in

₆
ages. _____ (she/work) much lately?

₇

Keiko: It says here that she _____ (take) some time off, but she's starting a new

₈
film next year.

Yuko: That's good news. I _____ (love) her last film.

₉

COMBINING FORM, MEANING, AND USE

6 **Thinking About Meaning and Use**

Choose two possible responses to complete each conversation.

1. **Gary:** Hanna just called. She's been sitting in traffic for over an hour.

   Peter: _____
   - **a.** I guess she's going to be late.
   - **b.** So that's why she was so late!
   - **c.** That's why she's been getting here late.
   - **d.** That's so frustrating!

2. **Lisa:** Oh, look. It's been raining.

   Sarah: _____
   - **a.** Don't forget your umbrella.
   - **b.** Try not to step in the puddles.
   - **c.** I'm glad it stopped.
   - **d.** You're right. It is.

3. **Yuji:** I've just been reading an interesting article about whales.

   Satomi: _____
   - **a.** Can I read it when you're done?
   - **b.** What does it say?
   - **c.** When did you write it?
   - **d.** Who's been writing it?

4. **Man:** How long have you been selling used cars?

   Car Dealer: _____
   - **a.** Six years ago.
   - **b.** Six so far.
   - **c.** For about a year.
   - **d.** Since 1998.

5. **Hector:** What's Carlos been doing lately?

   Silvio: _____
   - **a.** Taking lots of courses.
   - **b.** He's just studied really hard.
   - **c.** He's a full-time student these days.
   - **d.** He's fine.

6. **Father:** Has Sarah been having problems at school?

   Mother: _____
   - **a.** Yes, she has. She's very upset.
   - **b.** No, she isn't. Everything's fine.
   - **c.** No, but she's been working really hard.
   - **d.** Yes, she has been there.

There are nine errors in this text. The first one has been corrected. Find and correct eight more.

The History of Soccer

Soccer is the most popular international team sport. Historians believe that people ~~has~~ *have* been playing soccer since the year 217 A.D., when the first game has been part of a victory celebration in England. Soccer became popular in Europe over the centuries, and eventually it spread throughout most of the world. In the United States, soccer has always been being secondary to American football. Recently, however, soccer has growing in popularity.

In 1904, several nations have formed the International Federation of Football (FIFA), which has been regulating international competition since over a century. Since 1930, the World Cup have been bringing countries together. And although women weren't playing soccer for as long as men have, an important international event, the Women's World Cup, has been taken place every four years since 1991.

On a separate sheet of paper, write two paragraphs about an activity that you have been involved in for several years. It could be learning English or an academic subject, or a sport or favorite pastime, such as playing soccer or playing a musical instrument. Use the present perfect continuous, the present perfect, and the simple past when possible.

1. In the first paragraph, write about how long you have been doing this activity and describe your feelings about it in general.

2. In the second paragraph, write about your experience in more detail. Answer questions such as these:

   • Have you been doing this activity continuously over the years, or have you done it for a short time, then stopped, then started again, etc.?

   • Have you improved or learned quickly enough?

   • Have you ever felt frustrated with your progress?

   • What "lessons" have you learned that might be interesting to another person interested in that subject or activity?

> Playing soccer is one of my favorite activities. I have been playing soccer ever since I was five years old. I like it because . . . .

The Past Perfect and the Past Perfect Continuous

FORM

Examining Form

Read this excerpt from a romance novel and complete the tasks below.

> $\mathcal{J}$ulie <u>had been walking</u> for hours when she suddenly noticed that the sun was sinking low in the sky. She ⟨had lost track⟩ of time because she had been thinking about the most important decision she'd ever had to make in her life.
>
> Things hadn't been the same between Julie and her fiance, David, since he accepted
> 5 a job in Paris. They had known each other for almost five years, and in that time, they had never argued much. Lately, though, their relationship had become stormy. They seemed to be finding fault with each other and disagreeing about everything. For the first time, she was starting to wonder if she was ready for marriage. And with the wedding only twenty days away, she needed to make up her mind soon.
>
> 10 Everything in Julie's life had been going well until her world fell apart just a month before. A large company had offered David an important position that would require him to move to France. As his wife, Julie would have to go, too. Why hadn't he discussed his decision with her?
>
> Although Julie had always wanted to live abroad, she felt very confused. Was she
> 15 ready to move halfway across the world, leaving behind her friends and family and the only home she had ever known? If the answer was no, was she ready to say goodbye to the only man she had ever loved?

1. There are three examples of the past perfect continuous in the story. The first one is underlined. Underline two more.

2. There are many examples of the past perfect. The first one is circled. Circle six more.

3. How are the past perfect and the past perfect continuous different in form? Check all the correct statements below. Correct the incorrect statements.

   _____ **a.** The past perfect uses two auxiliaries.

   _____ **b.** The past perfect continuous uses two auxiliaries.

   _____ **c.** Both the past perfect and the past perfect continuous use *have* or *has* to form contractions, negative statements, and short answers.

Before Stefan went away to college, he had never done these things. Write sentences about Stefan, using the words in parentheses and the past perfect.

Before this year,

1. (cook his own meals) _he had never cooked his own meals._

2. (wash his own dishes) _____

3. (make his own bed) _____

4. (do his own laundry) _____

3 Practicing the Past Perfect Continuous

A community group organized a project to clean up a park. How long had the group been working when the people below came to help? Look at the list and write sentences in the past perfect continuous.

```
RIVERSIDE PARK CLEANUP SCHEDULE

 9:00-10:00   pick up the trash
10:00-10:30   pull weeds
10:30-11:00   wash the benches
11:00-12:00   paint the benches
12:00-12:30   clean the playground
12:30- 1:00   rake leaves
```

1. Ana got there at 9:15. _When Ana got there, the group had been_
   picking up the trash for fifteen minutes.

2. Chris and Emily arrived at 10:25. _____

   _____

3. Sasha came at 10:35. _____

   _____

4. Jane got there at 11:30. _____

   _____

5. Mr. and Mrs. Rivera came at 12:20. _____

   _____

6. Rick arrived at 12:45. _____

   _____

The Past Perfect and the Past Perfect Continuous   37

MEANING AND USE

 Ordering Events in the Past

Look at the timeline of Pablo Picasso's life. Then read each pair of sentences about Picasso and combine them, using the adverb in parentheses and the past perfect.

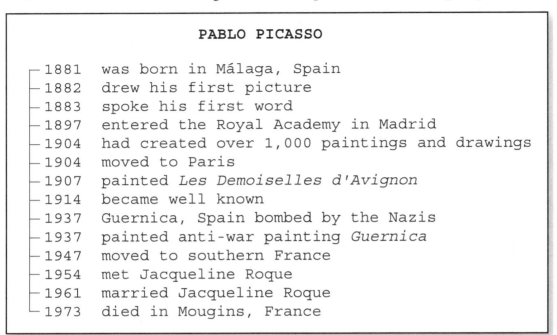

PABLO PICASSO

1881	was born in Málaga, Spain
1882	drew his first picture
1883	spoke his first word
1897	entered the Royal Academy in Madrid
1904	had created over 1,000 paintings and drawings
1904	moved to Paris
1907	painted *Les Demoiselles d'Avignon*
1914	became well known
1937	Guernica, Spain bombed by the Nazis
1937	painted anti-war painting *Guernica*
1947	moved to southern France
1954	met Jacqueline Roque
1961	married Jacqueline Roque
1973	died in Mougins, France

1. Picasso drew his first picture.

   Picasso turned two. (by the time)

   Picasso had drawn his first picture by the time he turned two.   OR

   By the time he turned two, Picasso had drawn his first picture.

2. Picasso spoke his first word.

   Picasso drew his first picture. (before)

   _____

   _____

3. Picasso lived in Málaga.

   Picasso entered the Royal Academy in Madrid. (until)

   _____

   _____

4. Picasso was 23 years old.

   Picasso produced more than 1,000 works of art. (by the time)

   _____

   _____

5. Picasso became well known.

   Picasso moved to Paris. (after)

   _____

   _____

6. Picasso painted *Les Demoiselles d'Avignon.*

   The history of art changed forever. (after)

   _____

   _____

7. The Nazis bombed Guernica, Spain.

   Picasso painted his anti-war painting, *Guernica.* (after)

   _____

   _____

8. Picasso moved to southern France.

   Picasso lived in Paris for many years. (when)

   _____

   _____

9. Picasso and Jacqueline Roque got married.

   Jacqueline Roque was Picasso's companion for seven years. (before)

   _____

   _____

10. Picasso lived in Mougins for almost 20 years.

    Picasso died. (when)

    _____

    _____

A. The community group from Exercise 3 continued working after lunch. Look at their plans for the afternoon.

```
            FINAL RIVERSIDE PARK CLEANUP SCHEDULE

 9:00-10:00   pick up the trash      2:00-2:30   cut the grass
10:00-10:30   pull weeds             2:30-3:30   trim the trees
10:30-11:00   wash the benches       3:30-4:30   plant flowers
11:00-12:00   paint the benches      4:30-5:00   empty the trash
12:00-12:30   clean the playground               cans
12:30-1:00    rake leaves
 1:00-2:00    LUNCH
```

B. Write sentences describing what the group had already done and what they hadn't done yet when the following people got to the park. Use the past perfect with *already* and *not . . . yet* and the words in parentheses.

1. Nancy arrived at 10:30. (pick up the trash/wash the benches)

   The group had already picked up the trash, but they hadn't washed

   the benches yet.

2. Susan and Jeff got there at 11:00. (cut the grass/pull weeds)

   _____

   _____

3. The Castro family arrived at 12:00. (rake leaves/pick up the trash)

   _____

   _____

4. Diane and Eric arrived at 3:30. (plant flowers/trim the trees)

   _____

   _____

5. The Hassan family arrived at 4:30. (empty the trash cans/plant flowers)

   _____

   _____

Expressing Reasons and Contrasts

Match the different words or phrases from each column to write twelve logical sentences with the past perfect and the past perfect continuous.

		I'd been working at the computer for hours.
		I'd left my glasses at home.
		my old one had been running fine.
I bought a new car		I hadn't worked very hard on it.
My eyes were aching		I'd been studying very hard.
My teacher loved my report	although	I'd taken a nap after lunch.
My grades were terrible	because	I hadn't been taking good class notes lately.
I'd never bought a new car		I'd never had enough money.
I got a low grade on my report		my parents had always promised to help with the payments.
		my old one had been acting up.

1. <u>I bought a new car although my old one had been running fine.</u>

2. _____

3. _____

4. _____

5. _____

6. _____

7. _____

8. _____

9. _____

10. _____

11. _____

12. _____

COMBINING FORM, MEANING, AND USE

7 **Thinking About Meaning and Use**

Choose two possible endings to each sentence.

1. We didn't see Bill at the party because
   a. he'd left before we arrived.
   b. he left after we got there.
   c. he got there after we'd left.
   d. we arrived before he went home.

2. Maria got a terrible sunburn
   a. because she had used plenty of sunscreen.
   b. even though she had stayed in the shade.
   c. although she hadn't used sunscreen.
   d. because she'd spent the day at the beach.

3. I'd been driving for hours,
   a. but I'm not ready to stop.
   b. and I'd never felt so tired.
   c. and I was starting to feel sleepy.
   d. so the car has run out of gas.

4. By the time the police came,
   a. an ambulance took the man to the hospital.
   b. a large crowd of people had gathered.
   c. the firefighters have put out the fire.
   d. we'd all managed to get out of the car.

5. Eric had been sleeping late
   a. before he got this job.
   b. after he got this job.
   c. because he was tired from work.
   d. although he was tired from work.

6. Rachel had never seen a live tiger
   a. after she went to the zoo.
   b. before she went to India.
   c. until she traveled to Africa.
   d. when she'd gone on safari.

8 **Writing**

On a separate sheet of paper, write a three-paragraph story about a recent event in the lives of two people (husband and wife, boyfriend and girlfriend, people in a family). Follow the format of the story in Exercise 1. Use the past perfect, the past perfect continuous, the simple past, and time clauses to describe the setting and to explain the story.

1. In paragraph 1, introduce one of the people. Where is that person, and what is he or she thinking about?
2. In paragraph 2, introduce the second person and talk about the event. How has that event affected the relationship?
3. In paragraph 3, talk about the person's feelings and how the person plans to deal with the event.

> Jake had been driving in the rain for over an hour when suddenly he realized what he had to do. Over the past two weeks, he had tried too hard to control the situation. Now . . . .

Chapters 4–6

A. Use the cues to write sentences with the verb form in parentheses. If you can't write a correct sentence with that verb form, write (✗). Use contractions when possible. Then answer the question about each group of sentences.

> How long / the police / try / to solve that crime ?

1. _____
   (present perfect continuous)

2. _____
   (past perfect continuous)

3. _____
   (present perfect)

4. _____
   (simple past)

5. *In which sentence(s) are the police no longer trying to solve the crime?* _____

> We / shop / at that store for years .

6. _____
   (past perfect)

7. _____
   (simple past)

8. _____
   (present perfect continuous)

9. *In which sentence(s) is the store probably out of business?* _____

> They / have / that car since 1998 .

10. _____
(present perfect)

11. _____
(past perfect)

12. _____
(present perfect continuous)

13. _____
(past perfect continuous)

14. _____
(simple past)

15. *In which sentence(s) do they still have the car?* _____

B. Match each sentence with the response below.

_____ **16.** I've been working out for over an hour.

_____ **17.** My parents had been living in the same house since 1980.

_____ **18.** We hadn't been waiting long for Lee and Kalysa when they came.

_____ **19.** I'd been exercising for almost two hours.

_____ **20.** Have you always wanted to be a doctor?

_____ **21.** My family has lived in the same house since I was born.

_____ **22.** When I looked out the window, I saw that it had rained.

---

a. I'm surprised you didn't hear the rain. It didn't rain for long, but it was loud.

b. No, I wanted to be a lawyer.

c. Why did they move?

d. You were lucky, because they're usually late.

e. Aren't you exhausted?

f. They'll probably live there forever.

g. I'm sure you were exhausted.

C. Check (✓) the sentences that are correct. Write (x) next to the sentences that have errors in form or meaning and use and rewrite them.

23. _____ Jenny has been walking for hours when she noticed it was late.

_____

_____

24. _____ I didn't see Rosa because she'd left before I arrived.

_____

_____

25. _____ Yuji is been cooking all day for the party.

_____

_____

26. _____ Until we went to France last summer, we've never eaten snails. They're delicious!

_____

_____

27. _____ Gary has been in love with Kate since he first saw her.

_____

_____

28. _____ Alex won the perfect-attendance award because he hadn't been missing a day since school started.

_____

_____

29. _____ The American Revolutionary War had lasted from 1775 to 1783.

_____

_____

30. _____ By the time we got to the Grand Canyon, we'd been driving for ten hours.

_____

_____

7 Modals of Possibility

FORM

Read this magazine article and complete the tasks below.

Computer Viruses Can Strike at Any Time

Victor decided to check his e-mail once more before he left the office for the day. He <u>might</u> have a reply from his supervisor about the two personal days that he wanted to take the following week. When he looked, there was only one message in his mailbox. The subject line read ILOVEYOU. "Who could that be from?" thought Victor, who rarely
5 received personal e-mail at work. "Someone's got to be playing a joke," he decided as he double-clicked on the attached document. Too late! Victor had just opened a file containing a dangerous computer virus that was later referred to as the Love Bug. Less than a second later, everything on Victor's hard drive had disappeared.

A deadly virus like the Love Bug could strike at any time. So how do we protect
10 ourselves? Here is some advice from the experts:
- Don't open e-mail from strangers. That message from "A FRIEND" might contain a virus that could cause you major headaches.
- Back up important files on a regular basis. That way, it should be easy to replace them if a virus wipes out your hard drive.
15 • Install the latest anti-virus software. It may not be possible to protect your computer against every brand-new virus, but keeping your software up to date ought to give you some peace of mind.

---

back up: make a copy of
double-clicked: clicked twice with a mouse
hard drive: the part of a computer that stores information

install: make ready for use
subject line: topic of message
wipes out: destroys

1. There are many examples of modals and phrasal modals in the article. The first one is underlined. Underline six more. Some will be used more than once.

2. What follows the modals? Check all the correct answers below.

_____ **a.** base form of the main verb

_____ **b.** infinitive of the main verb

_____ **c.** *be* + verb + *ing*

Working on Modals of Possibility

Check each sentence for the correct form of the modals and phrasal modals of possibility and probability. If the sentence is incorrect, correct it.

	CORRECT	INCORRECT
1. Blind dates must ~~be~~ be very nerve-wracking.		✓
2. This article has to be correct.		
3. I mayn't be in class tomorrow.		
4. They should be here by now.		
5. Should the accused man be innocent?		
6. This hasn't got to be right. It makes no sense.		
7. Could these keys be Amy's? Yes, they could be.		
8. Steve must feels terrible about this.		

3 **Completing a Dialogue with Modals of Possibility**

Complete these conversations using the words in parentheses. Use contractions when possible.

Conversation 1

    Koji: It's almost 8:00. Where <u>could Alex be</u> (Alex/be/could)?
                                        1

Tomiko: He really _____ (be/ought to) here by now.
                             2

    Koji: Well, _____ (he/be/can/not) sick. I spoke to him a little while
                       3

    ago, and he was fine.

Tomiko: He _____ (be/may) stuck in traffic. Let's wait a few more
                4

    minutes.

    Koji: If we wait much longer, _____ (we/miss/might) the beginning
                             5

    of the movie. Oh, there's the phone. _____ (that/be/have to) Alex.
                                   6

Tomiko: I hope so, but where _____ (he/be/call/could) from?
                              7

    Koji: He just got a cell phone. _____ (he/be/call/must) from his car.
                           8

Conversation 2

Kim: Oh, no! _____ (this/be/happen/can/not)! It sounds like
              ¹
          _____ (we/be/running out of/might) gas.
              ²

Nancy: _____ (how/that/be/could)? We just filled the tank.
              ³

Kim: I know, but the gauge shows that we're almost on EMPTY.

Nancy: The gauge _____ (be/have to) wrong.
                          ⁴

Kim: Maybe. Or there _____ (be/could) a hole in the gas tank.
                              ⁵

Nancy: That would explain it. Well, _____ (we/be/should)
                                              ⁶
          close to Route 70. There _____ (be/ought to) a gas station there.
                                        ⁷

MEANING AND USE

4 Expressing Degrees of Certainty

Read these sentences and complete the task below.

1. The cake ought to be ready. It's been in the oven for an hour.

2. There may be life on Mars, but most scientists doubt it.

3. She could have the flu, or she could just be tired.

4. There must be an easier way to clean this floor. Let's try using a brush.

5. Tony might be right about the court date.

6. This number can't be right. There's no such area code as 123.

7. David couldn't be guilty of such a terrible crime. I've known him all his life, and he wouldn't hurt a fly.

8. That's got to be Diane Waters's laptop. The screen says "Welcome, Diane."

9. This must be the house. I'm pretty sure that's Gary's car parked in front.

10. It's really sunny out this morning. It should be a beautiful day.

In the sentences above, find the following:

a. three examples that express a guess about a present situation (little certainty):
   2,_____

b. two examples that express an expectation about the present (some certainty):

   _____

c. three examples that draw a conclusion (strong certainty): _____

d. two examples that express the belief that something is impossible (strong

   certainty): _____

Complete the conversations with appropriate modals. Use *could, might* or *may* (little certainty); *should* and *ought to* (some certainty); or *must, have to,* or *have got to* (strong certainty). In some of the sentences, more than one answer is possible.

1. **Elena:** Are the cookies done yet?

   Teresa: They __might__ be. The recipe says to bake them for twelve to fifteen minutes, and they've been in the oven for almost fourteen.

2. **Amy:** Aren't you worried about the traffic?

   Susan: Not really. It's only 3:00, so the traffic _____ be pretty good.

3. **Satomi:** I found these keys on the sofa. Are they yours?

   Keiko: No, but they _____ be Yuko's. I've found her keys there before.

4. **Chris:** Whose comic books are these?

   Matt: They _____ belong to Jeff. He's the only one we know who still buys comics.

5. **Ana:** We saw Rosa and Paulo at the movies last night. They were holding hands. Are they dating?

   Jane: They _____ be. Rosa told me she had a new boyfriend, but I didn't know it was Paulo!

6. **Kate:** There's someone at the door.

   Ben: That _____ be Tony. He was going to try to stop by on his way home.

7. **Silvio:** Do you think they've developed our film yet?

   Luisa: The pictures _____ be ready by now. They promised to have them for us yesterday.

8. **Rick:** Is this Gary's house?

   Steve: It _____ be. That's Gary's car parked in the driveway.

9. **Chen:** I don't have a watch. What time is it?

   Lee: It _____ be just after 8 P.M. because the sun is setting now.

10. **Keon:** Do you know the name of that beautiful girl in the red dress?

    Marcus: It _____ be Jada. I think I met her once.

Using Modals of Future Possibility

Rewrite the sentences. Use *could, might,* or *may* (little certainty); *should(n't)* and *ought to* (some certainty); or *will* or *won't* (strong certainty). There may be more than one correct answer.

1. It's very likely that it will be clear today.

   It should be clear today. OR It ought to be clear today.

2. There's a good chance that it will be cooler tonight.

   _____

3. It's possible that it will rain tomorrow.

   _____

4. There's a small chance that it will be warmer on Thursday.

   _____

5. There isn't any chance that it will snow on Saturday.

   _____

6. It's definite that the temperature will drop tomorrow.

   _____

COMBINING FORM, MEANING, AND USE

Thinking About Meaning and Use

Read each situation and look at the pair of sentences that follow. Write *S* if the two sentences have the same meaning. Write *D* if their meanings are different. For the sentences that are different, change the *b* sentence so that it means the same as *a.*

_D_ 1. Tony almost never takes medicine, but he just took two aspirin.

   a. He must have a really bad headache.

   b. He might have a really bad headache.

   He's got to   OR   He has to have a really bad headache.

_____ 2. Mary lost her job today.

   a. She must be upset.

   b. She might be upset.

   _____

_____ **3.** You should probably start dinner without me.

     a. I may be late tonight.

     b. I will be late tonight.

_____ **4.** I haven't heard from Sarah in over a week.

     a. She's got to be really busy.

     b. She must be really busy.

_____ **5.** The sky is getting very dark.

     a. It could rain any minute.

     b. It should rain any minute.

_____ **6.** We're still making our vacation plans.

     a. We may go to Hawaii.

     b. We might go to Hawaii.

_____ **7.** I heard a strange rumor about Koji today.

     a. It couldn't be true.

     b. It can't be true.

_____ **8.** We're going to the Santana concert tonight.

     a. It should be great.

     b. It may be great.

_____ **9.** There's the sign: "Bill's Diner."

     a. This has to be the place.

     b. This ought to be the place.

_____ **10.** I'm not exactly sure where Kevin is, but

     a. he might be in his room.

     b. he could be in his room.

There are nine errors in this student's e-mail. The first one has been corrected. Find and correct eight more.

To: Lanita Carter
From: Matt Kennedy
Cc:
Subject: next week

Hi, Dr. Carter. I'm writing to tell you that I probably ~~mightn't~~ *won't* be in class next week. My grandfather may needs an operation, and my parents want me to come home to be with the family. No one has told me yet what kind of surgery Grandpa needs, but it should be serious. Otherwise, my family wouldn't be suggesting that I make the long trip home. You'll may find this a bit unusual, but I'm very close to my grandfather. I know this absence could to put my grade in danger, but I'll work very hard so that I don't fall behind.

You mayn't be very happy about this, but I need to ask a special favor. Do you think you might being able to e-mail me next week's assignments? That way, I maybe able to do some of them while I'm away. I'm not sure, but I should am getting back to Los Angeles by April 1.

Thank you very much.

Matt Kennedy

On a separate sheet of paper, write a two- or three-paragraph letter to someone — a teacher, a friend, a relative, or your boss. Follow these steps:

1. Think of a situation where you are supposed to do something in the future but can't. Make notes for a letter in which you explain why.

2. Use your notes to write your letter. Remember to express your ideas with the correct verb tenses and present and future modals of possibility.

I wanted to tell you why I won't be able to lend you my car next week. I have to make a short business trip . . . .

---

8 Past Modals

FORM

Read this excerpt from a history book and complete the tasks below.

Mystery in Malta

The small Mediterranean island of Malta is covered with grooves–thick lines that cut into the bare rocks, some as deep as 24 inches (600 mm). They run in pairs across the landscape and disappear into fields, roads, or houses, over cliffs and even into the sea.

5   Where <u>could</u> these grooves <u>have come</u> from? One theory was that the grooves were used to drain water. Experts decided to rule this out, however. The grooves couldn't have been part of a drainage system because they show no sign of water erosion.

  Another possibility is that the grooves may have been an ancient civilization's 10 transportation system. Although wheeled vehicles couldn't have used them because the pairs of grooves are not exactly parallel, some archaeologists think that a type of primitive sled must have provided transportation for the inhabitants of Malta in about 2000 B.C. The problem with this theory: Who or what could have pulled the sleds? Animal hooves would have worn down the 15 rock, and even bare feet would probably have polished the surface. But apart from the grooves themselves, there aren't any other marks. The "Maltese Mystery" continues to fascinate both archaeologists and tourists.

---

1. There are eight examples of past modals in the excerpt. The first one is underlined. Underline seven more.

2. Check the correct statements about past modals.

_____ **a.** Past modals have only one form with all subjects.

_____ **b.** Past modals have this form:

modal + *have* + past participle of main verb.

Rewrite these sentences, using the past modal form. Use the time expressions in parentheses. Make all necessary changes.

1. I should take a coat to the game tonight. (last night)

   I should have taken a coat to the game last night.

2. I could pick you up at the airport tomorrow. (last weekend)

   _____

3. The students might not understand everything on today's test. (yesterday's)

   _____

4. David must be at the office right now. (yesterday afternoon)

   _____

5. We could go to the mountains this summer. (last summer)

   _____

6. There may be a lot of traffic this afternoon. (this morning)

   _____

7. The company might solve its financial problems this year. (last year)

   _____

8. You shouldn't stay up late tonight. (last night)

   _____

Complete these conversations using the words in parentheses. Use contractions when possible.

Conversation 1

Kedra: Eva _should have been_ (be/should) here an hour ago. She's never late.
　　　　　 1

　　　　 What _____ (happen/could) to her?
　　　　　　　　　　 2

Jane: She _____ (might/not/receive) my message. I called to tell
　　　　　　　　　　 3

　　　　 her we were coming here instead of going to Sugar and Spice. She

　　　　 _____ (must/go) to Sugar and Spice.
　　　　　　 4

Conversation 2

Derek: The police think they _____ (might/catch) the
Boonton Burglar.
₁

Keon: It's about time! They _____ (should/got) him months ago.
₂

It _____ (should/not/take) this long. That guy
₃

_____ (had to/be/laughing) at the police since he started
₄

robbing houses.

MEANING AND USE

4 Using Modals of Past Possibility

Read these sentences about "unexplained mysteries." Then rewrite the ideas, using
modals of past possibility and the cues in parentheses. In each sentence more than
one modal is possible.

1. Amelia Earhart was the first woman to fly across the Atlantic. She tried to fly around the world
but disappeared. Did she have an accident, or is that just what she wanted people to think?

   a. She landed safely on an island and lived there. (guess)

   She might have/could have/may have landed safely on an island and
   lived there.

   b. She secretly returned to the United States. (guess)

   _____

   c. She ran out of fuel and crashed. (logical conclusion)

   _____

2. Stonehenge is a group of prehistoric stones in England. No one is sure what it is or
why it was built.

   a. The builders traveled over land and sea to bring the stones for the monument.
   (logical conclusion)

   _____

   b. The building of the monument didn't start before 3000 B.C. (unlikely or
   impossible)

   _____

   c. The structure was a temple. (guess)

   _____

5 Expressing Disbelief About the Past

Imagine that some students told the class they had these experiences. Write two sentences giving your response, the first one expressing disbelief. Use the modals in parentheses.

1. "We saw Elvis Presley last night." (could, must)

   a. _They couldn't have seen Elvis because he's been dead for many years._

   b. _They must have seen someone who looked like Elvis._

2. "We've finished the homework." (could, may/start)

   a. _____

   b. _____

3. "The trip from New York to Washington, D.C., takes about three hours by train. We got there in less than an hour." (can, might/less than three hours)

   a. _____

   b. _____

4. "Rick robbed the bank."
   (could, someone else/must)

   a. _____

   b. _____

5. "We won a million dollars in the Publisher's Contest. We didn't receive an advertisement."
   (can, must/advertisement)

   a. _____

   b. _____

6. "The President called us. He wants us to visit him in the White House."
   (can, must/joke)

   a. _____

   b. _____

7. "Kim cooked a three-course meal by herself. Her mother didn't help."
   (can, must/help)

   a. _____

   b. _____

8. "Lee completed the race in under an hour."
   (could, might/an hour and a half)

   a. _____

   b. _____

Expressing Advice and Obligations About the Past

Read this story and write your advice about what went wrong in this bank robbery.
Use *should have, shouldn't have,* or *ought to have.*

Several employees of a large factory decided to rob a bank a few blocks from the factory. The group thought the police would never look for them at the factory, so they went back to work after committing the crime. One problem: They had forgotten to remove their identification badges during the robbery.

1. They shouldn't have robbed a bank so close to their job.

2. _____

3. _____

4. _____

Expressing Regrets About the Past

Read the lists that describe Mr. O'Connor's regrets about the past—both the things that he did and the things that he didn't do. Complete the statements Mr. O'Connor would make about his regrets. Use *should have* or *shouldn't have* and phrases from the chart.

Things He Did	Things He Didn't Do
get married so young	exercise more
work so hard	take better care of his teeth
skip his medical checkups	learn to control his temper
live in the same town all his life	go to college

1. I shouldn't have lived in the same town all my life , but I didn't want to move.

2. _____ , but your grandmother and I fell madly in love.

3. _____ , but I hated going to the dentist.

4. _____ , but I never liked studying that much.

5. _____ , but I was too lazy to go to a gym.

6. _____ , but I had to earn enough money for my family.

7. _____ , but it's difficult to control.

8. _____ , but I was scared of doctors when I was younger.

COMBINING FORM, MEANING, AND USE

8) Thinking About Meaning and Use

Choose two possible responses to complete each conversation.

1. **Jake:** I ought to have heard from my brother by now.

   Peter: _____
   a. What did he say?
   b.) What time was he supposed to call?
   c. Has he called you yet?
   d.) He might have forgotten.

2. **Ana:** Mmm. Something smells good.

   Rosa: _____
   a. Dad must have cooked dinner.
   b. Grandma should have made cookies.
   c. My sister must bake a cake for her cooking class.
   d. Mom may have fixed her famous spaghetti.

3. **Carlos:** Could Peter have come by while we were out?

   Gary: _____
   a. Yes, I guess he could.
   b. Yes, he might have.
   c. Yes, he may have been.
   d. No, he couldn't have.

4. **Tomek:** Weren't you supposed to start your new job last Monday?

   Teresa: _____
   a. No. I didn't have to start until Wednesday.
   b. Yes. I must have started on Monday.
   c. No. I shouldn't have started on Monday.
   d. Yes. And I did.

5. **Kedra:** It's Bill's birthday. Should I have gotten him something?

   Marcus: _____
   a. No, you must not have.
   b. No, you didn't have to.
   c. Yes, I think you were supposed to.
   d. Yes, you have to have.

6. **Soo-jin:** Wasn't Professor Chapman coming to the class party?

   Sun-hee: _____
   a. Should he have gone to a meeting?
   b. He should have forgotten about it.
   c. Could he have gotten too busy?
   d. He might have changed his mind.

7. **Celia:** We should have had dinner while we were downtown.

   Luisa: _____
   a. So you must not be hungry.
   b. I could have taken you to a nice restaurant on Main Street.
   c. Why were we supposed to have dinner downtown?
   d. You're right. I'm sorry that we didn't.

8. **Satomi:** Kim moved to San Francisco last month.

   Takeshi: _____ I saw her less than a week ago.
   a. She can't have moved.
   b. She ought not to have moved.
   c. She should have moved.
   d. She couldn't have.

Read the letter that Miguel wrote to Gina, an advice columnist, and complete the task below.

Dear Gina
by
Gina Burke

I have a problem with my wife, Marta. She is jealous of my old girlfriend, Diane. Diane and I dated in college. I used to think about marrying her, but I waited too long to ask (I think I was too shy), and she married someone else. After Marta and I got married, Diane got divorced. Well, soon after, Diane and I had lunch together a few times. I didn't think Marta would approve, even though Diane and I are just friends, so I told her I was with my friend Steve. Marta found out the truth and told me to stop seeing Diane. Well, I have promised not to see Diane anymore, but I would like to know what I should have done. Was I wrong to see her? Should I have told my wife? What could I have done differently? I feel pretty confused right now.

—*Miguel G.*
San Jose, CA

Imagine that you have received this letter while Gina is on vacation and you must write an answer for Gina. On a separate sheet of paper, write a one-paragraph answer to Miguel. Tell him what he should or shouldn't have done or how he could have done things differently. Use *might have*, *could have*, *should have*, and *shouldn't have* when possible.

> Boy, Miguel, you are confused. I think you're the problem here, not your wife. First of all, you shouldn't have lied to her about seeing Diane . . . .

Chapters 7–8

A. Rewrite these sentences, choosing from the modals in the box. Do not change the meaning. Use each modal only once and change the form as necessary.

can't	ought to
could	has got to
might	shouldn't
may not be	should

1. I heard on Channel 7 that we might have a severe storm tonight.

   _____

2. You could have grown taller if you had eaten your spinach at every meal.

   _____

3. It must be very difficult for you to see your friend sick.

   _____

4. He ought to have been here an hour ago.

   _____

5. I'm fairly certain this won't take more than about five minutes.

   _____

6. That rumor about Rick couldn't possibly be true!

   _____

7. We really should call Paulo tonight.

   _____

8. Maybe she isn't coming to class today.

   _____

B. Read each situation. Then rewrite the sentences, using modals to express the meaning in parentheses. There may be more than one correct answer.

> Hiro has been working overtime a lot lately.

9. He needs the money. (possibility)

_____

10. He's saving for a new car. (conclusion)

_____

11. Hiro's boss is grateful. (obligation)

_____

12. Hiro is exhausted. (understanding)

_____

> I was calling Teresa for hours last night, but the line was busy.

13. She took the phone off the hook. (past possibility)

_____

14. She was talking to her boyfriend. (logical conclusion about the past)

_____

15. Her phone is out of order. (guess)

_____

16. She wasn't on the phone that long. (disbelief about the past)

_____

> Kate just got her driver's license.

17. She isn't old enough to drive. (disbelief)

_____

18. She had a birthday recently. (guess about the past)

_____

19. She drives carefully. (advice)

_____

C. Circle all the possible words or phrases to complete each sentence.

20. Kate is getting married next month. She _____ very excited.
    - **a.** could be
    - **b.** must be
    - **c.** might be
    - **d.** can be

21. Bill went home early today. He _____ well.
    - **a.** must not have felt
    - **b.** must not be feeling
    - **c.** mustn't feel
    - **d.** must not feel

22. Paul is not answering the phone. He _____ away.
    - **a.** should be
    - **b.** must be
    - **c.** can't be
    - **d.** might be

23. Nancy isn't here yet. _____ she have gotten stuck in traffic?
    - **a.** Should
    - **b.** Ought to
    - **c.** Must
    - **d.** Could

24. Should Mr. Ponce have been at the meeting this morning? Yes, _____ .
    - **a.** he could have
    - **b.** he should have
    - **c.** he should have been
    - **d.** he could

25. The police have very little doubt: The Bayside Burglar _____ guilty of the crime.
    - **a.** has to be
    - **b.** must be
    - **c.** might be
    - **d.** can be

26. The students in Mrs. Costa's class must stand up when they want to speak, but we _____ stand in our class. We're allowed to stay seated.
    - **a.** may not
    - **b.** mustn't
    - **c.** don't have to
    - **d.** can't

27. There's a story in the paper about a man who says he was kidnapped by tiny gray men with huge eyes. The man _____ .
    - **a.** should see a doctor
    - **b.** must be crazy
    - **c.** is probably lying
    - **d.** has got to have a vivid imagination

28. Chris had his cellular phone, so he _____ us. Why didn't he?
    - **a.** could call
    - **b.** might have called
    - **c.** should be calling
    - **d.** could have called

29. I'm tired of that song. I _____ it twenty times already on the radio today.
    - **a.** might be hearing
    - **b.** 've got to have heard
    - **c.** have to hear
    - **d.** must have heard

30. What do I think of the story? Well, it sounds pretty silly, but I guess it _____ true.
    - **a.** can be
    - **b.** could be
    - **c.** might be
    - **d.** should be

9 Passive Sentences (Part I)

FORM

1 Examining Form

Read this article and complete the tasks below.

Exploring the Mind/Body Connection Through Flotation Therapy

When flotation therapy <u>was</u> first <u>used</u> extensively in the 1990s, people were surprised by some of the results. One of the things that was discovered was the link between sensory deprivation and the emotions.

When they are being given flotation therapy, people <u>are shut</u> in a dark soundproof box
5 where they float in a tank of water. Most input is removed from their senses, but the senses are never entirely shut off. People listen to music or watch videos inside their tanks. In these circumstances, floaters experience deep tranquility and peace.

When *all* sensory output is removed, however, people have an experience that is far from relaxing. This was first proven by a group of psychologists at McGill University in
10 Canada.

In the McGill experiment, student volunteers were placed in padded clothing and put into completely soundproof chambers of water. Their eyes were covered, and their ears were plugged. The students were told that they could stay as long as they wanted. A panic button was their connection to the outside world while they were being
15 observed by the psychologists running the experiment.

Most students experienced strong negative emotions during the course of the experiment. They pressed the panic button after a few hours and refused to return to the isolation tanks. They said that while in the tank, they were visited by terrifying visions.
20 It isn't clear why humans react so negatively to extreme sensory deprivation. One theory is that the brain starts to dream because it thinks the body has gone to sleep. Since the body is actually wide awake, these dreams sometimes appear as frightening visions.

---

1. There are four examples of the simple present passive in the article. The first one is underlined. Underline three more.

2. There are many examples of the simple past passive. The first one is underlined twice. Draw two lines under five more.

3. Circle one example each of the present continuous and past continuous passives.

A. Complete this paragraph with the simple present passive form of the verb in parentheses.

Mardi Gras, or Fat Tuesday, _is celebrated_ (celebrate) in many cities around the
<u>1</u>
world in late February or early March, but Mardi Gras in New Orleans, Louisiana,

_____ (consider) by many to be the most spectacular. During the week
<u>2</u>

before Fat Tuesday, the French Quarter of New Orleans _____ (fill) with
<u>3</u>

long, winding parades. These parades _____ (make up) of magnificent floats
<u>4</u>

and marching bands. Spectators _____ (entertain) by a variety of performers.
<u>5</u>

Plastic bead necklaces and a variety of toys _____ (throw) from the floats,
<u>6</u>

and these "treasures" _____ (catch) by the spectators lining the parade route.
<u>7</u>

The parades _____ (enjoy) by thousands of people.
<u>8</u>

B. Now rewrite the paragraph above using the simple past passive.

Last week, Mardi Gras, or Fat Tuesday, was celebrated in many cities

around the world, but Mardi Gras festivities in New Orleans, Louisiana . . .

_____

_____

_____

_____

A. Complete this paragraph from an environmental report written about 20 years
ago. Use the present continuous passive form of the verb in parentheses.

Africa's Lake Victoria _is being choked_ (choke) by a plant. The beautiful water
<u>1</u>

hyacinth _____ (blame) for causing serious ecological damage. Bays
<u>2</u>

_____ (turn) into muddy swamps. As a result, boats _____
<u>3</u>   <u>4</u>

(trap), and breeding grounds for mosquitoes _____ (create).
<u>5</u>

The water hyacinth had never grown in Victoria until about fifteen years ago,

and no one knows how it got there. Because of the plant's floating leaves, harbors

_____ (block). The pipes at a power station _____ (clog).
<u>6</u>   <u>7</u>

Fishing _____ (threaten) as well.
<u>8</u>

B. The water hyacinth problem in Lake Victoria is much less serious these days. Rewrite the preceding paragraph in the past continuous passive.

In the 1980s and 1990s, Africa's Lake Victoria was being choked

by a plant. The beautiful. . . .

_____

_____

_____

_____

MEANING AND USE

4 **Focusing on Agents or Receivers**

Create active or passive sentences in the simple present or simple past. Use the words given. The first words in each item must be the subject of your sentence. In some sentences, more than one answer is possible.

1. the mail/deliver/at 11:00/every day _The mail is delivered at 11:00 every day._

   OR The mail was delivered at 11:00 every day.

2. the study/complete/last month

   _____

3. the children/not eat/breakfast/this morning

   _____

4. the house/clean/the housekeeper/once a week

   _____

5. the accident/occur/last Sunday

   _____

6. our house/destroy/the flood/a year ago

   _____

7. many tourists/visit/our city/in the summer

   _____

8. the employees/allow/leave early/on Fridays

   _____

A. Look at the verbs in these active sentences. Check (✓) whether each verb has only an active form or also a passive form.

	HAS ONLY AN ACTIVE FORM	HAS A PASSIVE FORM
1. The city recently built a new parking garage.		✓
2. Parking was becoming a serious problem.		
3. Cars were filling up the parking lots by 11:00 A.M.		
4. Construction of the garage cost a million dollars.		
5. The city is also putting in a park near the garage.		
6. The park has a rose garden.		
7. A landscaping company is planting the rose bushes.		
8. Many people now visit the park during lunch hour.		
9. A photo of the park appeared in today's newspaper.		
10. The newspaper also published an article about the park.		
11. The company grows all kinds of roses.		
12. Workers downtown appreciate the improvements.		

B. Look again at the sentences above. Change them to the passive if possible. If a sentence cannot be changed to the passive, write an X.

1. _A new parking garage was recently built by the city._

2. _____

3. _____

4. _____

5. _____

6. _____

7. _____

8. _____

9. _____

10. _____

11. _____

12. _____

Complete the sentences using a verb from the box. If a sentence requires a passive form, change the verb to the passive. Change active verbs to the simple past when necessary. Some of the verbs may be used more than once.

bring	choose	destroy	sing
fall	kill	watch	play

1. During World War II, many buildings in London _were destroyed_ by bombs.

2. The world's best athletes _____ together every four years at the Olympic Games.

3. The International Olympic Committee _____ Athens as the site of the 2004 games.

4. Do you ever wonder how a city _____ as the site for the Olympics?

5. Natural disasters _____ thousands of people every year.

6. The Berlin Wall _____ on November 9, 1989.

7. That important event _____ by people all over the world.

8. People all over the world _____ the moon landing on July 16, 1969.

9. How many of us witnessed the explosion of the *Challenger* shuttle on January 28, 1986, when everyone on board _____ ?

10. The Internet _____ together computer users all over the world.

11. The World Cup _____ by hundreds of millions of people all over the world.

12. Over 5,000 people _____ during the earthquake in Kobe, Japan in January, 1995.

13. "Happy Birthday" _____ on a person's birthday.

14. Judy Garland _____ "Somewhere Over the Rainbow" in the musical film, "The Wizard of Oz."

15. The famous jazz musicians John Coltrane and Miles Davis _____ together for several years.

16. Every time a Frank Sinatra song _____ on the radio, my mother cries.

COMBINING FORM, MEANING, AND USE

Read each sentence and the statements that follow. Write *T* if the statement is true, *F* it is false, or *?* if you do not have enough information to decide.

1. The visitors were asked not to smoke.

    __?__ **a.** The visitors asked us if they could smoke in the building.

    __T__ **b.** We asked the visitors to put out their cigarettes.

    __T__ **c.** Smoking is not allowed in our building.

2. Our neighbors' house is being remodeled now.

    _____ **a.** The remodeling has already started.

    _____ **b.** The remodeling is already finished.

    _____ **c.** The neighbors are remodeling it themselves.

3. Luisa is being picked up at the airport.

    _____ **a.** We don't know who's picking her up.

    _____ **b.** Someone has already picked her up.

    _____ **c.** She's picking up another person.

4. The package was sent to my aunt.

    _____ **a.** My aunt sent the package.

    _____ **b.** Someone sent her a package.

    _____ **c.** She hasn't received it yet.

5. When we arrived, the bridge wasn't destroyed yet.

    _____ **a.** Someone destroyed it before we arrived.

    _____ **b.** Someone destroyed it after we arrived.

    _____ **c.** We arrived before someone destroyed it.

6. The directions are written in the letter.

    _____ **a.** Someone already wrote the directions.

    _____ **b.** Someone is writing the directions.

    _____ **c.** We already read the directions.

There are eight errors in this student's composition. The first one has been corrected. Find and correct seven more.

>   Animal groups are ~~classifying~~ *classified* according to their basic structure. For billions of years, animals have kept certain features that are use to identify them. For example, all mammals have backbones and are warm-blooded. These features are also seen in birds.
>
>   The whale is a special case. A whale is often mistaken for a fish; it is actually a mammal. Originally, all mammals were lived on land. Their bodies were keeping warm by a covering of hair, and they walked on four legs. They breathed air through nostrils into their lungs. Whales, like other mammals, lived on land, but they later adapted to living in water. Whales are cover with a thick coat of fat, or blubber. Thanks to their blubber, their bodies are kept warm, and the animals can tolerate very low temperatures.

A killer whale

Imagine that a natural disaster struck your town or area within the recent past. The disaster could be an earthquake, a flood, or a terrible storm. On a separate sheet of paper, write two paragraphs describing how your town or area was affected when the disaster happened, and how it is still influenced by the event. Use passive sentences when possible.

1. In the first paragraph, write about the effects of the disaster. How many buildings were destroyed? What areas were most affected? What happened to the people? Were they forced to leave? How were their lives changed by the disaster?

2. In the second paragraph, describe the present situation. Has your town or area returned to normal? Are some of the buildings still being repaired? Is life for some of the people permanently changed because of the event?

> My town was hit by a flood several years ago. Not many buildings were destroyed, but a lot of homes near the river were damaged. For example . . . .
>
> These days the town is being rebuilt. However, the town is still affected economically . . . .

10 Passive Sentences (Part II)

FORM

Read this letter and complete the tasks below.

 Midwestern Edison
4512 Commercial Street
Chicago, IL 60661

```
Ms. Carol Baker                    Past due: $37.23
4398 Cedar Street                   Current: $35.28
Chicago, IL 60614                      Total: $72.51

Dear Customer:

This bill is now due and payable. This is not a new bill but a
request for services that have already been billed.

Your utility service will be disconnected if the past due payment
5 is not made in thirty days.

Payment can be made at any of our local offices, by mail or by
phone. A fee will be charged for credit card transactions.

If an extension agreement is made but not kept, your service may
be shut off without further notice. If payment has already been
10 made, thank you, and please disregard this notice.

Sincerely,
```

1. There are eight examples of passive forms in the letter. The first one is underlined. Underline seven more.

2. Write two examples from the letter of each passive form in the correct category below.

   a. present perfect passive <u>have (already) been billed</u>

   b. future passive _____

   c. modal passive _____

Rewrite these sentences in the passive without an agent.

1. We should see children but not hear them.

   Children _should be seen but not heard._

2. We will not tolerate this type of behavior.

   This type of behavior _____

3. The technicians can't repair my computer.

   My computer _____

4. We've got to do something about the noise.

   Something _____

5. They need to rewrite the regulations.

   The regulations _____

6. They might not publish the book.

   The book _____

7. The authorities must find and arrest this criminal.

   This criminal _____

8. We will notify you if we accept your nomination.

   You _____

9. The police might give you a ticket.

   You _____

10. They should not penalize students for this.

    Students _____

11. The painters will paint the room tomorrow.

    The room _____

12. They might stop you if you try to go in without a ticket.

    You _____

Rewrite the newspaper headlines below using the present perfect passive. Add missing words, including articles.

1. Man Killed in Traffic Accident

   <u>A man has been killed in a traffic accident.</u>

2. Energy Company Caught in Scandal

   _____

3. Fireman Honored with Medals

   _____

4. Captives Freed in UN Rescue Operation

   _____

5. $4.4 Million Budget Approved

   _____

6. National Wildlife Reserve Endangered by Fire

   _____

7. Drug Company Fined in Lawsuit

   _____

8. President Asked to Sign Education Bill

   _____

9. New Cancer Drug Approved by Government

   _____

10. Baseball Added to Olympic Sports

    _____

11. $3.5 Million Raised for Brazilian Rainforest

    _____

12. Swimmer in Florida Bitten by Shark

    _____

MEANING AND USE

4) Including or Omitting Agents

Find five more sentences below where the agent does not need to be mentioned, and cross out the *by* phrase.

1. The book was written ~~by the author~~ in ten days.

2. This book was written by the author of *Moon Rising*.

3. The fish is caught and frozen immediately by the fishermen to maintain freshness.

4. Our company was started by a young entrepreneur with a vision.

5. The woman was arrested by the police and taken into custody.

6. These photos were taken by some journalists at the war front.

7. Because of the holiday, no mail will be delivered by the letter carrier on Thursday.

8. I think my watch has been stolen by a thief.

9. Chris is going to be interviewed by someone half his age.

10. The pilot was given clearance for takeoff by the control tower.

5) Understanding the Passive in Academic and Public Discourse

Read the numbered excerpts below. Write the letter of the probable source next to each.

_a_ 1. An albatross, rarely seen in the North Atlantic, has been spotted in the New York metropolitan area.

____ 2. The president is elected by popular vote every four years, and may be reelected only once.

____ 3. Children must be supervised at all times. Running and shouting are not allowed in the pool area.

____ 4. If payment is not received within seven days, your account will be placed with a collection agency.

____ 5. The number you are calling has been changed. The new number is area code 718–663–7806.

____ 6. Iron and steel bars are heated to 900 degrees Fahrenheit; then the two metals are joined using a power hammer.

a. a newspaper report

b. a science magazine

c. an encyclopedia

d. a recorded announcement

e. a public notice

f. a formal letter

COMBINING FORM, MEANING, AND USE

6 Editing

There are eight errors in this article. The first one has been corrected. Find and correct seven more.

The mapping of the human genetic code has been called the most important scientific advance of our time. It will be transformed medicine beyond recognition. New drugs will develop for previously untreatable diseases, and ways will found to replace or repair faulty genes. Treatments will be matched to an individual's genetic make-up and doctors will be able to predict the future of their patients with much greater certainty.

Some cancers will be disappeared completely, and eventually, inherited diseases may wipe out by removing faulty genes from the gene pool.

However, many people believe that genetic information can use by insurance companies and employers to discriminate against people on medical grounds. In a speech praising the scientists, the President warned that genetic information must never used to segregate, discriminate against, or invade the privacy of human beings.

7 Writing

On a separate sheet of paper, write two paragraphs about a recent problem in your community. Use present perfect passives, modal passives, and future passives when possible.

1. In your first paragraph, describe the problem and how your community has been affected by it.

2. In the second paragraph, describe how the problem will be solved by your community.

In my community, the Sereno Bridge has been closed for repairs, and the traffic is terrible. The bus drivers have also been on strike, so it is difficult for people to get to work. . . .

The Sereno Bridge will be reopened soon by the Mayor. The bus drivers' strike will also be solved since the bus drivers will be given a salary increase. . . .

CHAPTER

11 Contrasting Gerunds and Infinitives

FORM

1 Examining Form

Read this story and complete the tasks below.

> When I was six years old, my mother took me to school on opening day. Sometime during that first day, a small boy started <u>to cry</u>. I immediately went over to him and put my arms around him to comfort him. The teacher ordered me to go back to my seat. I couldn't believe the teacher's indifference; in
> 5 my home I was used to (being) hugged whenever I cried.
>
> The teacher kept telling me to leave the boy alone, and I kept refusing to obey her until the boy stopped crying. I went home that day with a note to my mother that said I was rude, disobedient, and a troublemaker.
>
> The next day my mother came back to school to talk to my teacher. She
> 10 said that she had taught me to be considerate and warm towards others and that I was not likely to change. She advised my teacher to get used to my sympathetic nature.
>
> That incident happened 72 years ago, and I have enjoyed hugging a lot of people since then.

1. There are nine examples of infinitive forms in the story. The first one is underlined. Underline eight more.

2. There are five examples of gerund forms. The first one is circled. Circle four more.

Complete the sentences with one of the phrases in the box. Use capital letters when necessary.

building a new library	to go camping this weekend
having a plan for the future	to play with matches
learning a new language	to teach math
parking in a bus zone	to surf the Internet

1. <u>Having a plan for the future</u> _____ is important.

2. _____ will cost a lot of money.

3. It's dangerous _____ .

4. _____ takes time and patience.

5. _____ is illegal.

6. It isn't difficult _____ .

7. It would be fun _____ .

8. It can't be easy _____ .

Complete these sentences using one of the verbs in parentheses. Change the verbs to gerund or infinitive forms, as appropriate.

A. (*learn, take, go*)

We're going to Hawaii on vacation next month. I'm really looking forward to

_____<u>taking</u>_____ it easy for a change. I also want to spend some time
1

_____ how to use a surfboard. When I'm at home, I never have
2

time _____ to the beach.
3

B. (*make, understand, speak*)

When Keiko first came to the U.S., she found it hard _____
1

Americans. She wasn't used to _____ with people in English.
2

Now she has no trouble _____ herself understood when she
3

wants to.

C. (*go, click, shop*)

Shopping on the Internet has made our lives a lot easier. It's now possible

_____ at home instead of _____ to a store.
         1   2

The amazing thing is, you can buy whatever you need just by

_____ a mouse!
         3

D. (*give, start, get*)

Kevin's car wasn't running very well. He was having trouble

_____ it in the morning, and it was costing him a lot of money
         1

for repairs. In the end, he wound up _____ it to a friend. He
                                               2

wasn't sorry _____ rid of it, because he found a great deal on
                       3

another car.

MEANING AND USE

4) Understanding Verbs Used with Infinitives and Gerunds

Write *S* if the meaning of the two sentences is the same or very similar. Write *D* if the
meaning is different.

1. __D__ Can we stop watching the movie?

       Can we stop to watch the movie?

2. _____ The cleaners didn't start working until noon.

       The cleaners didn't start to work until noon.

3. _____ It will continue raining through the evening.

       It will continue to rain through the evening.

4. _____ I didn't remember locking the door.

       I didn't remember to lock the door.

5. _____ We regret to say that Mr. Jones died.

       We regret saying that Mr. Jones died.

6. _____ The roof has begun leaking.

       The roof has begun to leak.

7. _____ I tried to send a message on Ben's computer.

       I tried sending a message on Ben's computer.

8. _____ I'll never forget doing that.

       I'll never forget to do that.

Choose the correct answers to complete the sentences. In one case, more than one answer is possible.

1. I'll help you _____ that box. It's very heavy.
   a. lift   b. lifting   c. lifted

2. My parents won't let _____ MTV.
   a. me watch   b. to watch   c. me watching

3. Can you ask Gary _____ me a call when he comes back?
   a. give   b. to give   c. given

4. You can't make _____ vegetables if I don't want to.
   a. me eat   b. I eat   c. me to eat

5. Please put on a sweater when you go out. I don't want _____ cold.
   a. you get   b. to get   c. you to get

6. The teacher had _____ in groups for this project.
   a. the students work   b. the students to work   c. the students were working

7. Celia would like _____ some time off because her father is sick.
   a. take   b. to take   c. her mother to take

8. Don't ask _____ that. I can't understand a word of it.
   a. I translate   b. translating   c. me to translate

9. Would you make the kids _____ the TV?
   a. to turn off   b. turn off   c. turning off

10. I'll let _____ my new car if you promise to be careful.
    a. you driving   b. you to drive   c. you drive

11. I'm going to want _____ me a hand with this sofa. It's heavy.
    a. him to give   b. him give   c. giving

12. Coming to the U.S. has really helped _____ English.
    a. me learn   b. me to learn   c. me learning

COMBINING FORM, MEANING, AND USE

Complete the paragraphs with the appropriate form of the verb in parentheses. Use the gerund, the infinitive with *to*, or the infinitive without *to*. In **three** cases, two forms are possible.

You've worked hard all week. It's time _to enjoy_ (enjoy) life. You don't want
1
_____ (waste) time all weekend _____ (run) errands. The idea
2   3
of _____ (stand) in line at the supermarket fills you with horror. You
4
simply don't have the time _____ (go) to the post office. Or maybe you
5
just hate _____ (shop). But things need _____ (get) done.
6   7
Don't worry. Try _____ (use) a shopping service.
8

A growing number of companies exist _____ (meet) the needs of people
9
who are just too busy _____ (run) all their errands themselves. For fees
10
that start at $50 an hour, these companies provide a variety of services, from

_____ (register) their clients' car to _____ (clean) their house.
11   12

© 2000 Newsday, Inc. Reprinted with permission.

You write an advice column called "Dear Steve" for a newspaper. Read this letter that you have received. Then complete the steps that follow.

Dear Steve,

I am a twenty-six-year-old woman who has been dating a wonderful man for the past five months. Tony is very considerate and kind, and I am pleased that our relationship is growing more serious. There is, however, one problem that I am concerned about.

Tony is a reckless and aggressive driver. He often speeds and becomes very impatient with other drivers. He gets angry, makes faces and gestures, and he even curses at people who get in his way. When he is behind the wheel, he isn't the same sweet, loving person that I know. I've tried to talk to him about this, but he doesn't agree with me.

How can I convince Tony that he needs to change his behavior?

Confused

1. Think of some advice for this woman. On a separate sheet of paper, write sentences with gerunds and infinitives saying what she should do. Use some of the verbs in the box.

allow	avoid	tell	help	try
ask	consider	encourage	don't let	think about

2. Now combine your sentences into a letter responding to the woman. Develop your ideas with explanations and examples. Divide your advice into two or three paragraphs.

Dear Confused,

There are a number of things you could consider doing to deal with Tony's behavior. First, you could try telling him that you won't drive with him anymore . . . .

Chapters 9–11

A. Choose the correct words or phrases.

1. The magician cried "Abracadabra!" and the white rabbit _____.
   a. appeared   **b.** is appeared   **c.** was appeared

2. _____ home for the first time is often difficult.
   a. Leave   **b.** Left   **c.** Leaving

3. Many climbers _____ during an expedition in 1997.
   a. died   **b.** were died   **c.** are died

4. Why don't you take public transportation instead of _____ in a traffic jam every day?
   a. sit   **b.** sitting   **c.** sat

5. A prehistoric grave _____ in a cave in Turkey.
   a. has been finding   **b.** has been found   **c.** has found

6. Could you please get someone _____ me a call?
   a. give   **b.** giving   **c.** to give

7. When I went to open the window, I noticed that it _____ .
   a. breaking   **b.** was breaking   **c.** was broken

8. My girlfriend is always asking _____ her with her homework.
   a. me to help   **b.** to help   **c.** my help

9. My parents don't object _____ home late.
   a. to my coming   **b.** me to come   **c.** I come

10. We can't go in while the carpets _____ .
    a. are cleaning   **b.** are being cleaned   **c.** been cleaned

B. Complete the sentences using the gerund or infinitive form of the verb in parentheses.

I decided _____11_____ (take) up tennis as a way of _____12_____ (keep) fit. I planned _____13_____ (play) three times a week so I could get the maximum benefit out of it. But I found that I really enjoyed _____14_____ (meet) so many new people. I was interested in _____15_____ (make) friends while _____16_____ (wait) for a game. Soon I was spending more time _____17_____ (talk) to people than _____18_____ (play) tennis.

C. Rewrite the following sentences, using passive forms.

19. We encourage children in the United States to express themselves.

    Children _____

20. They will cancel the trip if the weather is bad.

    The trip _____

21. They founded the kingdom of Ethiopia around 1000 B.C.

    The kingdom _____

22. They're already advertising the next book in the series.

    The next book _____

23. We should recycle cans and bottles.

    Cans and bottles _____

24. They have done a lot of research in this area.

    A lot _____

D. Find and correct **one error** in each sentence.

25. I came to the United States for study English.

26. Martha's parents wouldn't let her to go out with her friends.

27. When I saw how much I had upset my sister with the news, I really regretted to tell it to her.

28. All students require to hand in their assignments on time.

29. Her father always wants that Lucy to help him when she wants to be with her friends.

30. The cost of living was increased a lot during the 1970s.

12 Indefinite and Definite Articles

FORM

1 **Examining Form**

Read this ad from a campus newspaper and complete the tasks below.

Travel Programs: French Language and Culture

Spend (the summer) living in the heart of Paris! While staying with <u>a family</u> or living near the Odéon in a
5 comfortable dorm, you will take a course in French culture while improving your knowledge of the French language. We plan a three-day weekend in Brittany, visiting charming Breton villages, plus day trips to Versailles and Rouen. In Paris, we will visit the theater and the
10 opera in the evenings, with visits to the Louvre and the Musée d'Orsay during the afternoons.

Louvre: world-famous art museum **Odéon:** a beautiful 18ᵗʰ century theater
Musée d'Orsay: museum of Impressionist painting

1. There are four examples of nouns with indefinite articles (*a/an*) in this ad. The first one is underlined. Underline three more.

2. There are ten nouns that are used with the definite article (*the*). The first one is circled. Circle nine more.

3. Find five nouns that are used with no article (Ø). Write them here.

   <u>programs,</u>

A. Write *a* or *an* before each of these noun phrases.

1. _an_ hour and a half   6. _____ usual thing

2. _____ half hour   7. _____ ugly shirt

3. _____ honest mistake   8. _____ U.F.O.

4. _____ university professor   9. _____ eventful day

5. _____ year abroad   10. _____ angry uncle

B. Read this list. Write *a* before the nouns when necessary. Write Ø if there is no article.

> ## CAMPING LIST
>
> 1. _a_ tent   6. ___ dishes
> 2. ___ sunscreen   7. ___ pocket knife
> 3. ___ cooking stove   8. ___ flashlight
> 4. ___ fuel   9. ___ soap
> 5. ___ insect repellent 10. ___ sleeping bag

MEANING AND USE

Complete the paragraph by writing *a*, *an*, or Ø before the nouns.

_____An_____ allergy is _____ immune response triggered by
_____1_____   _____2_____

sensitivity to _____ a substance such as _____ pollen,
              ___3___   ___4___

_____ dust, _____ chemicals, or even _____ food.
___5___   ___6___   ___7___

Contact with _____ substance can trigger _____ number of
             ___8___   ___9___

symptoms ranging from _____ skin rashes to asthma. _____
                      ___10___   ___11___

tendency toward _____ allergies often runs in _____ families,
                ___12___   ___13___

and heredity is thought to play _____ important role. Hay fever is one of
                                ___14___

the most common allergies, and it occurs when the immune system overreacts to

_____ pollen, which comes from _____ grasses,
___15___   ___16___

_____ trees, and _____ flowers.
___17___   ___18___

A. Decide why *the* is used in situations 1–3. Choose the correct reason from the box and write it in the space before each underlined noun.

> **a.** Mentioned Again: The item has already been mentioned.
>
> **b.** Visual Context: The listener can see the item.
>
> **c.** General Knowledge: The listener can guess which item the speaker means.

Situation 1

Could you give me some tomatoes? They're on the counter over there beside the bread box.

1. __b__ the counter

2. _____ the bread box

Situation 2

There was a truck on the road in front of me. I couldn't see very well because the truck was blocking my vision.

1. _____ the road

2. _____ the truck

Situation 3

I went to a musical performance last night. I didn't enjoy the recital very much. I liked the music all right, but the chairs were very uncomfortable.

1. _____ the recital

2. _____ the music

3. _____ the chairs

B. Decide why *the* is used in situations 4–5. Choose the correct reason from the box and write it in the space before each underlined noun.

> **d.** Familiar Nouns: The item is familiar to the speaker.
>
> **e.** Unique Nouns: There is only one.
>
> **f.** Noun Modifiers: The noun is modified.

Situation 4

I couldn't go to Emily's party because I was at <u>the hospital</u> with my son. We had to go to <u>the emergency room</u>. <u>The X-ray</u> showed he broke his leg.

1. _____ the hospital

2. _____ the emergency room

3. _____ the X-ray

Situation 5

When I came out of <u>the supermarket</u> this evening, my car didn't start because <u>the battery</u> had died. I called <u>the towing service</u> that I always use.

1. _____ the supermarket

2. _____ the battery

3. _____ the towing service

5 Choosing Definite or Indefinite Articles

Complete the paragraphs by writing *a, an,* or *the* before each noun. In one sentence more than one answer is possible.

A. Last summer I bought __*an*__ expensive pair of running shoes. But
$\overline{\hphantom{aaaa}1}$

shortly afterwards, my dog chewed _____ heel of one of them. So I took
$\overline{\hphantom{aaaa}2}$

it to _____ old shoe repair store on my street. I placed it on
$\overline{\hphantom{aaaa}3}$

_____ counter and told _____ man what had happened. He
$\overline{\hphantom{aaaa}4}$ $\overline{\hphantom{aaaa}5}$

picked up _____ shoe and looked at it. Then he placed it back on
$\overline{\hphantom{aaaa}6}$

_____ counter.
$\overline{\hphantom{aaaa}7}$

"Well, what do you recommend?" I asked.

The repairman looked at me and suggested "Give your dog _____
$\overline{\hphantom{aaaa}8}$

other shoe!"

B. One day I noticed my sister wasn't wearing _____ watch. When I asked
$\overline{\hphantom{aaaa}1}$

her why, she replied that she didn't need one. "At home there's _____
$\overline{\hphantom{aaaa}2}$

clock in every room and there's one in _____ car too," she replied. Since
$\overline{\hphantom{aaaa}3}$

she loves to shop, I asked her how she knew _____ time when she was
$\overline{\hphantom{aaaa}4}$

on _____ shopping trip. "That's easy," she said. "I buy something and
$\overline{\hphantom{aaaa}5}$

look at _____ time printed on _____ receipt."
$\overline{\hphantom{aaaa}6}$ $\overline{\hphantom{aaaa}7}$

Identify the underlined nouns in these sentences. Check (✓) *Generic* if the noun refers to a class of things or *Specific* if the noun refers to a particular thing.

	GENERIC	SPECIFIC
1. <u>Melons</u> are in the same botanical family as squashes.	✓	
2. <u>Orange-fleshed melons</u> are high in beta-carotene.		
3. Most of <u>the melons</u> in our market come from Texas.		
4. <u>The cantaloupe</u> is actually a muskmelon.		
5. I <u>bought</u> a cantaloupe on sale.		
6. <u>The cantaloupe</u> I had for breakfast was delicious.		

COMBINING FORM, MEANING, AND USE

There are nine errors in the paragraphs below. The first one has been corrected. Find and correct eight more.

Everybody likes ~~a~~ the sun, especially when there are the blue skies above. But we now know that even on the cloudy day in winter when you can't see a sun, rays of the sun are constantly attacking our skin. In fact, daily ongoing sun protection is an only way to stop wrinkles, because sun damage is the main reason we have wrinkles! So what you know about a sun protection today can literally save your skin.

During the summer, the sun's rays are strongest between 10 A.M. and 2 P.M. Clouds filter some of the rays, but not all, which is why you can still get burned on overcast day. Different surfaces such as a water, sand, or snow can reflect the rays of the sun so the hats offer only partial protection.

On a separate sheet of paper, write two paragraphs that describe your attitudes toward food and cooking. Use indefinite and definite articles as appropriate.

1. In the first paragraph, write about your attitudes toward food and cooking in general.

   • Is food important to you? Do you think about it a lot?
   • Do you think it's necessary to eat healthy foods? Why or why not?

2. In the second paragraph, write about your eating habits and describe some of the kinds of foods you like to eat.

   • What kind of food do you usually eat (e.g., Chinese, Mexican, or Italian food)?
   • Where do you eat most of the time? (e.g., fast food restaurants, your school's cafeteria, or at home)? If you eat at home, who cooks?
   • How many times a week do you go to restaurants?
   • What is the name of your favorite restaurant?
   • What do you usually order there?
   • If you cook for yourself or others, what dish do you cook best?
   • What was your favorite dish growing up? Do you still like it?

> I really like to eat. I live in a dorm at school, so I have most of my meals in the school cafeteria . . . .

13

Relative Clauses with Subject Relative Pronouns

FORM

1 Examining Form

Read this newspaper article and complete the tasks below.

Some Surprising Facts about Food

Here are a few food (facts) that
may surprise you:

Oranges and orange juice
provide most of the vitamin C in
5 the diets of Americans. However,
there are many vegetables that
contain just as much vitamin C
as citrus fruits such as oranges
or grapefruit. For example, one
10 green pepper, or one cup of
cauliflower, broccoli or Brussels
sprouts contains as much
vitamin C as an average orange.

People who eat potatoes and
15 whole-grain bread lose weight
faster. That's because these are
lower-calorie foods that satisfy
your appetite. Other calorie-light
foods that help fill you up include
20 oranges, apples, grapefruit, and
popcorn.

Americans eat 50% more
protein than they need.
Americans regularly consume
25 more protein and fat than
Europeans and Japanese, who
get more of their calories from
fruits, grains, and vegetables.

Parsley, which is often used to
30 decorate dinner plates but
usually remains uneaten, is an
excellent source of beta-carotene
and vitamin C. It also contains
natural ingredients that freshen
35 your breath. So you can skip
dessert, but don't forget to finish
off your meal by eating the
parsley on your plate!

---

1. There are eight examples of subject relative clauses in the article. The first one is underlined. Underline seven more.

2. Circle the noun that each relative clause modifies. The first one has been done for you.

2 Combining Sentences with *Who*, *That*, or *Which*

Combine each pair of sentences. Use the second sentence in each pair to make restrictive relative clauses using *who*, *that*, or *which*.

1. I work in an office. It has a view of the park.

   I work in an office that has a view of the park.

2. The lady asked me to help her. She lives in the next apartment.

3. I inherited a Swiss watch. It belonged to my father.

4. Do you see the girl? She is wearing a long dress.

5. The cat often visits me. The cat lives next door.

6. On the wall there are some photos. They have faded in the sun.

7. Try out the chair. The chair has a velvet back.

8. A warbler is a very small bird. It sings beautiful songs.

Working on Verb Agreement in Relative Clauses

Complete each sentence with an appropriate relative pronoun and the correct form of the verb in parentheses.

1. Do you know the man _who/that is wearing_ (wear) the black beret?

2. My sister, _____ (love) shopping, spends a lot of money on clothes.

3. Sarah wears shoes _____ (make) her look a lot taller.

4. The Clothes Rack, _____ (have) a store in our neighborhood, sells used clothing.

5. I bought a leather jacket _____ (be) on sale.

6. I'm the kind of person _____ (prefer) to wear casual clothes.

7. Bill decided to wear his gray suit, _____ (hang) in his closet.

8. I have a friend _____ (dress) like a fashion model.

MEANING AND USE

4 **Identifying Restrictive and Nonrestrictive Relative Clauses**

Underline the relative clauses in the sentences below. Use commas to punctuate the nonrestrictive clauses.

1. Last summer, I went to visit my great-aunt Luisa, <u>who is 96 years old</u>.

2. We stayed with a cousin who lives nearby.

3. My cousin's children who often visit my aunt came with us.

4. My aunt lives in an apartment building which is a historical landmark.

5. Her room which is on the ground floor has a view of the gardens outside.

6. When we arrived we spoke to her neighbor who has known her for a long time.

7. Aunt Luisa who is almost blind didn't recognize us at first.

8. But she got along well with my husband who comes from her home state.

9. Even though she can no longer drive she has an old Volkswagen that still looks brand new.

10. It's painted "sunshine yellow" which is a very bright color.

Combine the pairs of sentences using nonrestrictive relative clauses.

1. You must meet my friend Nancy. She writes romantic fiction.

   You must meet my friend Nancy, who writes romantic fiction.

2. Lisa might give you a ride. She lives near you.

3. We went to Bodega. It's a small town on the coast.

4. My friend Gina knows about fractures. She used to be a nurse.

5. My computer is on sale for $799. It cost me $1,500 a year ago.

6. I really enjoyed the book *Taxi*. It's about cab drivers in New York.

7. My cousin Amy is moving to Alaska with her husband. She got married in September.

8. That house on Store Street is for sale. It was built in 1850.

COMBINING FORM, MEANING, AND USE

Rewrite each group of sentences as one sentence. Use restrictive and nonrestrictive relative clauses.

Babu Chhiri (1965–2001)

1. The mountaineering world was shocked to hear of the death of Babu Chhiri. He was a Sherpa. He climbed Mt. Everest in under seventeen hours.

   The mountaineering world was shocked to hear of the death of

   Babu Chhiri, who was a Sherpa who climbed Mt. Everest in

   under 17 hours.

2. Chhiri was a remarkable mountaineer. He reached the peak of Mt. Everest twice in fourteen days.

   _____

   _____

3. Chhiri came from a small village in the foothills of the Himalayas. He first began to climb Everest when he was a porter for the more experienced Sherpas. They guide foreigners up the mountain.

   _____

   _____

4. Chhiri ran an adventures firm. The firm organized climbs for foreign teams. Chhiri wanted greater respect for the Sherpas. The Sherpas earn comparatively little money for their work.

   _____

   _____

On a separate sheet of paper, write two paragraphs about a person who has influenced your life. The person could be a parent, a family member, a teacher, or a well-known personality. Use restrictive and nonrestrictive relative clauses when possible.

1. In the first paragraph, describe the person who influenced you.

   • How did you come to know the person?
   • What is his or her name? Age? Occupation? Relation to you?
   • Has this person been in your life a long time or a relatively short time?

2. In the second paragraph, write about the influence this person has had on you.

   • Why has this person been an important influence?
   • Has he or she influenced you in one way, or in more than one way?
     Give examples.

My father, who is 51 years old, has influenced me a lot. He has always been strict with me. He's the kind of person that . . .

My father has been an important influence in my life because . . . .

14 Relative Clauses with Object Relative Pronouns

FORM

1 Examining Form

Read this magazine article and complete the tasks below.

Grizzly Bears a Threatened Species

Grizzly bears, once a common sight in the Western United States, have been a threatened species for 25 years. From the estimated 50,000 (grizzlies) <u>that Western</u>
5 <u>settlers first saw 200 years ago,</u> their numbers have dropped to 1,200 bears in just four states—Montana, Wyoming, Idaho and Washington.

These few remaining grizzlies now face a
10 threat biologists didn't foresee 25 years ago. Today, "modem cowboys" live in the country and work from their home computers. They have accelerated growth in the areas where the bears are found.

15   But "bears show up in places where bears have been for thousands of years," said Chris Servheen, grizzly bear recovery coordinator for the Fish and Wildlife Service. According to Servheen, residents in these areas need to learn the same lessons that campers in national parks have learned. Any garbage you have must be stored, any food that you leave around will attract
20 bears, and if you see an occasional bear show up in your backyard, it does not necessarily need to be killed.

1. There are seven examples of object relative clauses in the article. The first one is underlined. Underline six more.

2. Circle the noun that each clause modifies.

Combine the sentences, using the second sentence in each pair to make a restrictive relative clause. Practice different alternatives. In your first combination, use the relative pronoun *that*. In your second combination, omit the relative pronoun.

1. I bought the computer. The computer isn't working.

   The computer that I bought isn't working.

   The computer I bought isn't working.

2. They've sold the house. You liked the house.

   _____

   _____

3. This is the dish. The chef recommends it.

   _____

   _____

4. The woman gave me her number. I met the woman at the party.

   _____

   _____

5. Would you like to try on the dress? You saw it in the window.

   _____

   _____

6. Something made me sick. I ate something last night.

   _____

   _____

7. Would you like to see the car? I just bought it.

   _____

   _____

8. This is the wedding ring. My grandmother gave it to me.

   _____

   _____

Rewrite the following sentences. Make them less formal by omitting the object relative pronoun and moving the preposition to the end of the relative clause.

1. I found the book for which I was looking.

   I found the book I was looking for.

2. The movie about which I read is on TV tonight.

   _____

3. Hiro's the guy about whom I told you.

   _____

4. Kate really likes the people with whom she lives.

   _____

5. The car belongs to the woman for whom my husband works.

   _____

6. Send the letter back to the person from whom you got it.

   _____

7. At last, here is the news for which we've been waiting.

   _____

8. Is that the dog of which you're afraid?

   _____

Add a missing preposition to the end of each relative clause.

1. **Elena:** Eva is the only person I can talk ^to at school.

2. **Stefan:** Really? What about that girl you play basketball? The one you told me?

3. **Elena:** She's nice, but I don't like the people she hangs out.

4. **Rosa:** My friend Carlos got the job I applied at the bookstore.

5. **Yuko:** Really? Is Carlos the guy you used to work?

6. **Rosa:** Yes. He's the one I introduced you at the party.

7. **Mrs. Ruiz:** The house that the Smiths moved isn't as nice as their old one.

8. **Mr. Ruiz:** Yes, but the golf club they belong is right across the street.

MEANING AND USE

Choose a relative clause from the box to add information about each
underlined noun in the sentences below. Then rewrite each sentence. Add
commas when necessary.

> which I drank gratefully
> that we had seen by the side of the river
> that I lent you last week
> that we read last night
> that we saw on TV last night
> whom I loved dearly
> that I know at work
> which my father had built himself

1. A <u>guy</u> won the lottery.

   <u>A guy that I know at work won the lottery.</u>

2. Can you give me back the <u>money</u>?

   _____

3. Mom, please read me the <u>story</u>.

   _____

4. My aunt <u>Rosa</u> died last year.

   _____

5. The <u>program</u> was really interesting.

   _____

6. My aunt brought me some <u>tea</u>.

   _____

7. Our <u>house</u> stood at the top of a hill.

   _____

8. We stopped at a <u>campground</u>.

   _____

6 Using *Where* and *When*

Complete the sentences using your own ideas.

1. I live in a neighborhood where _everybody knows everybody else._ _____

   _____

2. Winter is the season when _____

   _____

3. I'll never forget the time when _____

   _____

4. In my house, the _____ is the place where _____

   _____

5. One of my favorite cities is _____ which _____

   _____

6. _____ is the place where _____

   _____

7. _____ is the year when _____

   _____

8. _____ is the day when _____

   _____

9. One of the best memories I have is the time when _____

   _____

10. New York City is the place where _____

   _____

COMBINING FORM, MEANING, AND USE

7 · Editing

There are ten errors in the article below. The first one has been corrected. Find and correct nine more.

Williams Sisters Started on Public Courts

Venus and Serena Williams, ~~that~~ *who* took the tennis world by storm in the late 1990s, began their careers on the public courts of Compton, California. Compton was a long way from the clubs that they would eventually play in the world's most prestigious tournaments. Tennis was not a popular sport for the neighborhood children, were fans of the LA Lakers basketball team. When the sisters were teenagers, most of the people they practiced were in their thirties and forties.

The girls soon began competitive play. But their father Richard who has been their coach since they were young, kept them out of the high-pressure tournaments who other girls played. According to the Women's Tennis Association rules, the number of tournaments a 16-year-old can play is fourteen. At that age, Venus played in just four.

It wasn't only burnout that the girls' parents worried. It was the pressures, that competitive tennis can place on a family. "Tennis doesn't make a family strong. It makes a family weak," says their father, which now oversees both girls' careers.

On a separate sheet of paper, write two or more paragraphs about friends or other groups of people. Use restrictive and nonrestrictive clauses when possible. Also try to use reduced relative clauses.

1. In paragraph 1, say which groups you will be writing about. For example, you may know one group of people you grew up with, another that you know at your current job or at school, and a third group that you go out to movies or dinner with now.

2. In your additional paragraph(s), describe each group briefly. Give examples of people who belong to each group.

> I have several groups of friends. For example, there are the friends I grew up with, the friends I . . . .
>
> I still have four or five friends from my childhood. John, who I have known since I was ten, ...

Chapters 12–14

A. Choose the correct word or phrase to complete each sentence. If nothing needs to be added, select Ø. In some of the sentences, more than one answer is possible.

1. There are _____ beautiful roses in the park this year.
   a. any
   b. Ø
   c. some

2. Who is the person _____ has influenced you the most?
   a. Ø
   b. that
   c. who

3. When you go to _____ Weiss Deli, could you buy some bread?
   a. a
   b. Ø
   c. the

4. The children soon forgot the country _____ they had left behind.
   a. Ø
   b. that
   c. who

5. A lot of college students carry _____.
   a. a cell phone
   b. cell phones
   c. the cell phone

6. Did you visit the house _____ Steinbeck lived?
   a. in which
   b. which
   c. where

B. Fill in the blanks with *a(n)*, *the*, or no article (Ø).

I am _____ nurse in _____ large hospital. One day,

7   8

_____ woman wearing _____ expensive jewelry came in for

9   10

_____ surgery. Before _____ operation, I itemized _____

11   12   13

rings, necklaces, and earrings she gave me and locked them in our safe.

Afterward _____ woman came into my office to collect _____

14   15

jewelry. When I put all _____ items on my desk to return to her, I was

16

surprised to see _____ gold earring that I hadn't seen before.

17

"Is this your earring?" I asked her.

"It's not _____ earring," she answered. "It's _____

18   19

thumb tack."

C. Find and correct **one** error in each sentence.

20. I gave the book to a friend of mine likes science fiction.

21. What's the name of the restaurant that all the rock stars go?

22. One day Dad came home with a large box, that he put on the top shelf of the
hall closet.

23. That's the same guy who he was working in the supermarket.

24. Susan wears black boots and a leather jacket that have several buttons missing.

25. My neighbor who had seen the accident was interviewed by the police.

D. Combine each pair of sentences, using the second sentence in each pair to make a
restrictive relative clause. Omit the object relative pronoun and use reduced forms
when possible.

26. I wanted to buy a present for a person. I like the person very much.

_____

27. So last Saturday I went to a mall. The mall is near my home.

_____

28. I was hoping to find a present. The present would not be too expensive.

_____

29. I had some money. I had saved the money from my part-time job.

_____

30. When I got on the streetcar, I saw a face. I recognized the face.

_____

15 Real Conditionals, Unreal Conditionals, and Wishes

FORM

1 ▶ Examining Form

Read this letter and complete the tasks below.

Your Medical Questions ─────────────

"Do I have agoraphobia?"

──────────────── by Rachel Curtis, M.D.

Dear Dr. Curtis:

Sometimes I think I'm crazy. Often I wish I were a different person. I've tried to find out what my problem is. 5 Someone told me that I might have agoraphobia.

What usually happens is this: <u>If I go to a place where there are lots of people, I panic.</u> Sometimes I get 10 dizzy and even faint. That's what happened to me when I went to a crowded movie theater not long ago. Soon after the show started, I began to feel very anxious. I thought my 15 feelings were silly, so I ignored them. I said to myself: If I just stay here and try to relax, everything will be fine. But then I got more and more frightened. Finally, I fainted and 20 they had to call an ambulance to take me to the hospital.

Some days I feel so anxious that I don't even go out of my apartment. Of course I wish I didn't react this way. 25 If I could just leave, I would be able to do the things I need to do. I would visit my friends. I could take a trip. I would start to enjoy my life again.

My friends don't really understand 30 my problem. If I tell them about it, they usually just say not to worry so much.

Please advise me. Do I have agoraphobia? If that is my problem, 35 then tell me what to do.

Yours truly,

(Name withheld)

Santa Barbara, CA

---

1. There are four examples of real conditionals in the article. The first one is underlined. Underline three more.

2. There is one unreal conditional. Circle it.

3. Draw a box around a sentence with *wish*.

A. Complete the real conditional sentences. Use the future with *will* (*'ll*) or the simple present form of the verb in parentheses.

1. If you don't have a bed, I <u>'ll sleep</u> (sleep) on the sofa.

2. My parents _____ (buy) me a car if I get good grades.

3. Where will you stay if you _____ (not/find) find a hotel?

4. If I _____ (do) my homework late at night, I remember it better.

5. If it _____ (keep) raining, you'll need an umbrella.

6. If I get a scholarship, I _____ (go) to a private college.

7. If André retires next year, he _____ (not/have) much money to live on.

8. Kim and I _____ (cook) the main course if you make dessert.

9. When will you get to the restaurant if you _____ (come) straight from work?

10. You _____ (have) more homework this weekend if you don't finish your essay now.

B. Complete the unreal conditional sentences. Use the conditional or the simple past form of the verb in parentheses.

1. If I weren't so busy, I <u>'d give</u> (give) you a hand.

2. If we _____ (have) a cell phone, we could call from anywhere.

3. What would your mother say if she _____ (see) you?

4. If he had his driver's license, he _____ (buy) a car.

5. Rita _____ (be) a better violinist if she practiced more.

6. If I _____ (tell) you, you wouldn't believe me.

7. More people _____ (study) in the library if there were more computers.

8. I wouldn't eat so many hamburgers if I _____ (think) they were bad for me.

9. If you _____ (lend) me your car, I would take good care of it.

10. The Johnsons _____ (buy) a house if they could afford it.

MEANING AND USE

3 **Expressing Warnings and Predictions with Real Conditionals**

Look at the pictures. For each one, use the cues to write two sentences about what will or might happen in that situation.

In the first sentence, use *if*. In the second sentence, use *unless*. Use real conditionals.

1. woman/put on sunscreen/get sunburned

   <u>If the woman doesn't put on sunscreen, she'll get</u>
   <u>sunburned. Unless she puts on sunscreen, she'll</u>
   <u>get sunburned.</u>

2. boy/eat the ice cream/fall on the floor

   _____
   _____
   _____

3. water skier/look out/hit/swimmer

   _____
   _____
   _____

4. woman/pay attention/purse/stolen

   _____
   _____
   _____

Using *Unless*

Complete the sentences using your own ideas.

1. You'll get sunburned unless <u>you put on some sunscreen.</u>

2. The staff won't work on Sundays unless _____

3. The plants will die unless _____

4. You won't get better unless _____

5. Don't call me unless _____

6. My children won't eat vegetables unless _____

7. We'll run out of gas unless _____

8. She will get fired unless _____

5 **Understanding Real and Unreal Conditionals**

Choose the correct response.

1. I wish we had more time.
    a. Yes. If we do, we can hike to the beach.
    b. Yes. If we did, we could hike to the beach.

2. We're all ready to go.
    a. Good. If we leave now, we won't be late.
    b. Good. If we left now, we wouldn't be late.

3. Diane's going to quit her job.
    a. Really? What will she do if she can't find another one?
    b. Really? What would she do if she couldn't find another one?

4. It's a pity your mother can't come.
    a. Yes. If she can come, she'll have a great time.
    b. Yes. If she could come, she'd have a great time.

5. I don't trust that politician.
    a. I agree. I'll vote for him if he's honest.
    b. I agree. I'd vote for him if he were honest.

6. I think I'll go to the party.
    a. Great! If you go, I'll go.
    b. Great! If you went, I'd go.

6) Asking for Permission with Unreal Conditionals

Rewrite the following questions. Use unreal conditionals to ask for permission.

1. Is it OK if I use a dictionary?

   Would it be OK if I used a dictionary?

2. Do you mind if I leave early today?

   _____

3. Is it OK if I come to see you in your office?

   _____

4. Do you mind if I'm late to class sometimes?

   _____

5. Does it bother you if I record the lectures?

   _____

6. Is it a problem if I give you the assignment on Monday?

   _____

7) Wishing About the Present and the Future

Complete the sentences using your own ideas.

1. I wish I had _more time to sleep every night._

   _____

2. If only I were _____

   _____

3. I wish my friends wouldn't _____

   _____

4. I wish my teacher would _____

   _____

5. If only the weather were _____

   _____

6. I wish you wouldn't _____

   _____

COMBINING FORM, MEANING, AND USE

8) Thinking About Meaning and Use

Complete the sentences with an appropriate affirmative or negative form of *have*. Use contractions when possible.

1. If we __had__ a lot of money, we'd buy a bigger house.

2. You _____ more energy if you exercised.

3. Would it be OK if we _____ the party outside?

4. If I _____ a moment this evening, I'll give you a call.

5. I _____ a soda if you have one with me.

6. I would come if I _____ so much work to do.

7. I can't see a thing! I wish I _____ my glasses with me.

8. If you _____ anything else to do, can you help me cook dinner?

9. He _____ an accident unless he drives more carefully.

10. If Koji doesn't come to the party, we _____ a ride home.

9) Writing

On a separate sheet of paper, write two paragraphs about how you could change two things about your life. Use real and unreal conditionals when possible.

1. In the first paragraph, list things in your life you would change. Would you stop procrastinating? Watch less TV? Live in a bigger house?

2. In the second paragraph, describe your choices with examples and illustrations.

> If I could change two things in my life, what would they be? Well, first, I would have a nice car. Right now I have to rely on friends for rides and use the buses and subway. . . .
>
> For my car, I would get a red Volkswagen. It would have a convertible top . . . .

16 Past Unreal Conditionals and Past Wishes

FORM

1 Examining Form

Read this magazine article and complete the tasks below.

A Premonition That Came True

Have you ever had a premonition—a feeling that you can predict the future? Here is an account of a premonition that came true.

I'm an actress, and one evening I was at a rehearsal for a play. My husband, Alex, called me on my cell phone on his way home from work. 5 He said he was going to stop at a convenience store to buy some milk and would pick me up after that. (My car was being repaired that day.)

For some reason, I really had the 10 feeling that he was in danger, and I told him not to stop at the convenience store. He laughed at me at first, but when I insisted, he agreed to come directly to the theater.

15 Later I found out the convenience store had been robbed by two young men at the time <u>Alex would have been</u> there. As they were escaping, one of them shot the cashier. Luckily 20 someone found him right away and took him to the hospital just in time.

I think about what happened a lot. If I hadn't listened to myself, our lives might have been very different. If Alex 25 hadn't listened to me, he would have walked in the door of the convenience store in the middle of the robbery. It's very possible the thieves would have shot him. If that 30 had happened, we wouldn't have had our son, and we wouldn't have bought a new house. It would have devastated me if he had been hurt … I don't even want to think about it. I 35 just wish the police had caught those two men. They never did.

---

1. There are seven examples of past unreal conditionals in the article. The first one is underlined. Underline six more.

2. Find a sentence that expresses a past wish and write it here:

_____

_____

Choose the correct word or phrase to complete each sentence.

1. Paulo _____ have gotten the job if he hadn't been late for the interview.

   a. will   **(b.)** would   **c.** should

2. If I'd known about the test, I wouldn't have _____ to school this morning.

   a. go   **b.** went   **c.** gone

3. If they _____ heard the weather forecast, they might have brought warmer clothes.

   a. had   **b.** would   **c.** have

4. It's Mary's fault. If she'd locked the front door when she left the house, we _____ been robbed.

   a. wouldn't have   **b.** wouldn't   **c.** would have

5. If you had _____ my advice, we wouldn't have gotten stuck in traffic.

   a. take   **b.** took   **c.** taken

6. What _____ done if you had been in this situation?

   a. would you have   **b.** have you   **c.** had you

7. If I'd told my parents about my decision, they _____ to stop me last week.

   a. would try   **b.** had tried   **c.** might have tried

8. Thank goodness you helped us! I don't know what we would have done if you _____ here.

   a. have been   **b.** hadn't been   **c.** wouldn't be

Identify whether the *'d* contraction in each sentence means *had* or *would*.

	HAD	WOULD
1. I wish I'd gone home earlier.	✓	
2. If Jake had been there, he'd have said something.		
3. If only we'd known!		
4. You wouldn't have enjoyed the concert if you'd gone.		
5. I'd have told you before, but I didn't know anything about it.		
6. If only you'd said something before now! We could have helped you.		
7. Would he have been accepted if he'd gotten better grades?		
8. They'd have told you by now if there were any openings.		

Working on Past Wishes

Match the beginning of each sentence with the correct ending.

1. It didn't rain at all last night. I wish _e_ .
2. They closed the freeway for repairs last month. I wish ____.
3. David didn't come to the party on Saturday. I wish ____.
4. I'm so sorry you weren't able to come. I wish ____.
5. I didn't study math in college, but I wish ____.
6. My friend Julie moved to Oregon last year. I wish ____.
7. I spent a lot of money on that dress. I wish ____.
8. We couldn't afford to rent that apartment, but I wish ____.

a. we could have
b. I hadn't
c. she hadn't
d. you could have
e. it had
f. he had
g. they hadn't
h. I had

MEANING AND USE

Using Past Unreal Conditionals

Rewrite the sentences, using *if* clauses and past result clauses. Begin each sentence with *if*. Use contractions when possible.

1. I didn't go to the party last night because I was tired.

   If I hadn't been tired, I would have gone to the party last night.

2. I was late because I overslept.

   _____

3. He didn't take a jacket, so he complained all evening about the cold.

   _____

4. Susan didn't know about the party, so she didn't go.

   _____

5. I didn't know what happened yesterday because I hadn't read the newspaper.

   _____

6. They didn't go camping because they didn't have a tent.

   _____

Choose the most appropriate response.

1. **Satomi:** I would have told you about the wedding if I'd known about it.

   Yuki: _____
   a. Oh! I thought you knew.
   b. Oh! I thought you didn't know.

2. **Matt:** I wish we'd left earlier.

   Sasha: _____
   a. Why? Are we going to be late?
   b. Why? Are we going to be early?

3. **Rick:** I would have come to the party if I could have.

   Steve: _____
   a. I hope you come.
   b. I'm sorry you missed it.

4. **Jada:** If I hadn't taken that vacation, we would never have met.

   Derek: _____
   a. Well, I'm sorry you didn't.
   b. Well, I'm glad you did.

5. **Ana:** If only they hadn't closed that swimming pool!

   Elena: _____
   a. Yes. The kids would have loved it.
   b. Yes. The kids will love it.

6. **Marta:** If we'd had more time, we could have stayed longer.

   Paulo: _____
   a. Yes. I'm sorry you have to leave.
   b. Yes. I was sorry you had to leave.

7. **Eric:** Our team would have won if Connor hadn't been injured.

   Gary: _____
   a. Yes. I'm sorry we lost.
   b. Yes. I'm glad we won.

8. **Maria:** I wish I hadn't bought this car.

   Gina: _____
   a. Really? Why didn't you buy it?
   b. Really? Why don't you like it?

Look at the pictures. For each picture, write a present wish sentence (refer to Chapter 15 if necessary) and a past wish sentence. Use contractions when possible.

1. (know someone here) <u>I wish I knew someone here.</u>
   _____

   (stay at home) <u>I wish I'd stayed home.</u>
   _____

2. (understand math better) _____
   _____

   (study harder) _____
   _____

3. (not be so late) _____
   _____

   (leave on time) _____
   _____

4. (can give someone else the check) _____
   _____

   (not offer to pay the bill) _____
   _____

COMBINING FORM, MEANING, AND USE

8 **Thinking About Meaning and Use**

Read these situations. Then use the cues to write two or three sentences about each situation. Use past unreal conditionals with *would*, *could*, and *might*. More than one answer is possible.

A. Jake didn't want to go to the party, but his friend Lee persuaded him to go. At the party, Diane, a beautiful woman from Texas, asked him to dance. Jake later married Diane. They are now living in Texas.

1. Jake (go) to the party/he (meet) Diane

   If Jake hadn't gone to the party, he wouldn't have met Diane.

2. Lee (persuade) Jake to go/he (dance) with Diane

   _____

3. Jake (meet) Diane/he (move to) Texas

   _____

B. A truck crashed into a bridge and spilled chemicals into the river. The chemicals polluted the river. As a result, the children didn't have a place to swim.

1. truck (spill) chemicals/chemicals (pollute) the river

   _____

2. truck (crash) into the bridge/the children (have) somewhere to swim

   _____

C. My parents left Honduras because of the war. My father had a cousin in Mexico, so they went there. His cousin worked in a hotel, and he found my father a job. My father bought the hotel after ten years. Now our family runs it.

1. there (be) war/my parents (leave) Honduras

   _____

2. my father (have) a cousin in Mexico/they (go) there

   _____

3. cousin (find) my father a job in a hotel/my dad (bought) the hotel

   _____

On a separate sheet of paper, write two paragraphs about an important event in your past or a decision you made and its effect on you. Describe what your life might have been like if circumstances had been different. Use past unreal conditionals and past wish sentences in your second paragraph when possible.

1. In the first paragraph, write briefly about the event or decision:

   • What was it?
   • Who was involved?
   • When was it?
   • How old were you at the time?
   • How did it affect your life?

2. In the second paragraph, write about what might have happened:

   • If it hadn't happened or you had made a different decision, what do you think would have been the result?
   • How do you think your life would have changed?

> When I was ten years old, my parents decided to move to California. We moved to Los Angeles in 1995, and my father went to work for . . . .
>
> If we hadn't come here, my life would have been very different. If we had stayed in our country, I wouldn't have learned English and . . . .

Chapters 15–16

A. Choose the most appropriate response.

1. Elena: If we had our swimming gear, we could go in the water.

Irina: _____

a. Yes, but we don't.

b. Yes, but we didn't.

2. Takeshi: If I'm on a short flight, I ask for a window seat.

Yuji: _____

a. So do I. I love to look out.

b. I didn't. I preferred the aisle.

3. Lee: We could make pancakes if we had more eggs.

Rita: _____

a. That's a good idea. Let's do that.

b. Would you like me to go and get some?

4. Chris: The neighbors are making a lot of noise again.

Keon: _____

a. I know. I wish they stopped.

b. I know. I wish they would stop.

5. Hector: It looks like rain. Maybe we'd better turn back.

Miguel: _____

a. Don't worry. If it rains, we'll take shelter.

b. Don't worry. If it rained, we'd take shelter.

6. Young-soo: Dennis shouldn't have acted so rashly.

Soo-jih: _____

a. I know. I wish he didn't.

b. I know. I wish he hadn't.

7. Andre: So were you late for your interview?

Stefan: _____

a. Yes, I was. I wouldn't be late if I took the car.

b. Yes, I was. I wouldn't have been late if I'd taken the car.

8. **Matt:** I wouldn't have called you if it hadn't been an emergency.

   Peter: _____

   a. Well, I'm glad you called.

   b. I wish you had.

B. Complete the sentences.

9. You _____ be late if you don't leave now.

10. Think of how much better life _____ be if cancer were cured.

11. I would _____ enjoyed the movie more if I'd been able to see the screen.

12. _____ you quit your job if you could afford to?

13. You'd sleep better if you _____ eat dinner so late.

14. The puppy _____ bite you if you don't annoy her.

15. The children will be upset if Grandma _____ come.

16. I _____ say anything if I were you.

C. Rewrite the statements as conditional sentences. Begin with the word(s) given. Do not change the meaning.

17. Many people will lose their homes unless something is done.

    If _____

18. I hadn't read the material, so I couldn't follow the lecture.

    If _____

19. The soccer team won the game because they practiced a lot.

    If _____

20. We won't get good seats if we don't arrive early.

    Unless _____

21. My grades were low because I didn't study.

    If _____

22. Conditions improved after the workers complained to the boss.

    If _____

23. I won't go to a party by myself if I don't know anyone there.

    Unless _____

24. You didn't listen to my advice, and you were sorry.

    If _____

D. Find the errors in the sentences of this conversation and correct them.

Peter:

25. "I'm an only child, and I wish I'm not.

26. If I have a brother or a sister, I can hang out with them.

27. Maybe they introduce me to their friends and I could get to know more people."

Lanita:

28. "I have five brothers and two sisters, so whenever I would need to talk, there is always someone to talk to.

29. One of my brothers or sisters could always help me out.

30. I can't imagine what my life will be like if my parents hadn't decided to have a large family."

17 Noun Clauses

FORM

1 Examining Form

Read this article from a college newspaper and complete the tasks below.

Internships Can Help Chart a Career Path

You like school, but you sometimes wonder <u>if your education (is going to be) useful in "the real world.</u>" You know that you want to work in marketing, but you have no idea what that really means. Or maybe
5 you just don't know what you want to be later on.

If any of this seems familiar, consider an internship—part-time paid or unpaid work in a company. An internship can help you get a clearer idea of where you might like to work, and it shows
10 future employers that you have a certain level of maturity and ambition.

An internship can also change your mind about your chosen career. After a summer spent working as an intern in an advertising agency, Grace Wong realized that she wanted to
15 move from computer science into public relations. Grace is now a successful advertising executive.

But an internship is hard work. According to Chris Kennedy, who worked for a major newspaper in Atlanta, Georgia, it's important to show employers that you work hard early on. That's when they're deciding whether or not they should
20 give you more challenging assignments.

If you would like to know how you can become an intern, there are many resources. . . .

1. There are many examples of noun clauses in the article. The first one is underlined. Underline six more.

2. Circle the verb or verb phrase in each noun clause.

Rewrite the following sentences, correcting the error(s) in each.

1. Can you tell me what time is it?

   <u>Can you tell me what time it is?</u>

2. Yuji isn't sure if or not he wants to be a doctor.

   _____

3. Do you remember what time did we leave?

   _____

4. Do you know that we have to pay or not?

   _____

5. I'd like to find out is that class required.

   _____

6. Have you decided that you're coming with us?

   _____

7. I wonder how can he do that.

   _____

8. I'm not sure what will I do.

   _____

9. Do you have any idea who was she?

   _____

10. I couldn't have known that it was a winning lottery ticket or not.

    _____

11. Could you explain what is the theory of relativity?

    _____

12. I wonder how many years has been this program on TV.

    _____

MEANING AND USE

Expressing Uncertainty

Complete the sentences with a logical ending. Use noun clauses.

1. I want to buy a new computer, but I need to figure out how much _it's_ _going to cost._

2. I knew my parents were talking about me, but I couldn't hear what _____

3. I'd like to study at Harvard, but it depends on whether _____

4. I was going to call you late last night, but I didn't know if _____

5. If you're upset about it, you should tell your friend how _____

6. We found a package in front of the door yesterday, but we don't know who _____

7. The bank will give us a loan, but they need to know how much _____

8. I had my umbrella a minute ago. Now I don't remember where _____

9. It's my grandmother's birthday today, but nobody knows how old _____

10. I'm really hungry, but I can't decide what _____

Asking Indirect Questions

Complete the indirect questions that you would ask in the following situations. Use *wh-* or *if/whether* clauses.

1. You'd like to use your electronic dictionary in class. You ask your teacher.

   I was wondering _if I could use my electronic dictionary._

2. You want to know the arrival time of the plane from Chicago. You ask the agent at the airport.

   Could you tell me _____

3. You're looking for the nearest post office. You ask someone on the street.

   I'm trying to find out _____

4. You're in a restaurant. You'd like to know the price of the dinner special. You ask the waiter.

   Can you tell me _____

5. You're looking at an apartment and would like to move in next week. You ask the owner of the apartment.

   I was wondering _____

6. You're interviewing a well-known actor. You'd like to know about his first acting jobs.

   Could you tell me _____

5) Understanding Tense Agreement

Choose one, two or three correct words or phrases to complete each sentence.

1. Oh, no! I forgot that I _____ a test today.
   (a.) have   **(b.)** had   **(c.)** am going to have

2. I know it _____ your birthday today because you told me.
   a. is   **b.** was   **c.** will be

3. I'm so sorry to disturb you! I didn't know you _____ there.
   a. are   **b.** were   **c.** will be

4. I brought my umbrella because I thought it _____ rain.
   a. will   **b.** was going to   **c.** would

5. The weather forecast says it _____ tomorrow!
   a. rains   **b.** rained   **c.** will rain

6. The scientist Isaac Newton always believed that white light _____ of many different colors.
   a. consists   **b.** consisted   **c.** will consist

7. We finally figured out that there _____ a water leak in the bathroom.
   a. is   **b.** was   **c.** had been

8. I didn't watch the movie because I thought I _____ it.
   a. see   **b.** saw   **c.** had seen

Rewrite the following sentences, changing the verb tense in the noun clause. Use the simple past, the past perfect, or *would*.

1. We've studied this before.

   I assumed _(that) we'd studied this before._

2. This is an easy assignment.

   I thought _____

3. The class will be easy.

   I believed _____

4. I won't have any problems passing.

   I was sure _____

5. You like that movie.

   I knew _____

6. You've seen it already.

   I thought _____

7. You want to see it again.

   I assumed _____

8. You'll go with me.

   I expected that _____

9. There won't be any delays at the airport.

   I was sure _____

10. He doesn't eat meat.

    I thought _____

COMBINING FORM, MEANING, AND USE

7 Editing

There are ten errors in the conversation. The first one has been corrected. Find and correct nine more.

Kim: Sarah, do you know where ~~is~~ my blue jacket? I don't know where I left it.

Sarah: I thought it's on the table.

Kim: No, it's not. By the way, do you know that the biology assignment is due tomorrow or on Monday?

Sarah: I believe it's due tomorrow.

Kim: Oh, no! Nancy said is due Monday! I thought I have the whole weekend. I'd better tell her. Do you know what's her number?

Sarah: I'm afraid not.

Kim: I wonder is she at Emily's house. You know, I really don't understand why do we have to do the assignment, anyway. Do you think is there going to be a test on it?

Sarah: I don't think so. I hope not! If there is, I'm not sure what I'm going to pass the class!

A. Think about your first experience in a new job, a new school, or a new country. Complete the sentences using your own ideas.

1. When I first came to / started to work in _____, I didn't know that

   _____

2. I couldn't understand why _____

   _____

3. I thought that _____

   _____

4. I didn't realize that _____

   _____

5. Now, I think that _____

   _____

B. On a separate sheet of paper, write a paragraph about your first experience in a new job, a new school, or a new country. Describe clearly how the experience changed your opinions or beliefs about something. Use the ideas from part A. Also, use noun clauses and correct tense agreement.

> When I started my first day in college, I didn't know that sometimes not all students can get the classes they want because the classes are full . . . .
>
> Now I realize that I should register early for classes to get the best teachers . . . .

18 Reported Speech

FORM

1 Examining Form

Read this newspaper article and complete the tasks below.

Bag Holding $67,432 Recovered

Mayor Tom Tavares yesterday thanked a young taxi driver for returning a bag holding $67,432 to its rightful owner.

5 <u>The taxi driver</u>, 21-year-old Ahmed Al-Said, (said) that he had picked up an elderly woman, Gwen Stephens, 76, at Star of the Sea Church on Sunday and taken her to 10 her home on Gregory Street. After the woman left, he noticed the bag of cash on the back seat, and took it to the police.

The woman told police that she 15 had closed her bank account and that she always carried her money with her because she was afraid of burglars.

She was overjoyed when police 20 returned the bag, which contained her life savings, and she asked to meet the taxi driver in person. When she asked the young man if he wanted a reward, he said that he 25 was just doing his job. He then advised the woman to put the money in a bank.

---

1. There are six examples of reported speech in the article above. The first one is underlined. Underline five more.

2. Circle the reporting verb in each sentence. The first one is circled.

A police officer is investigating reports of the sighting of an unidentified flying object (UFO). Read the quoted statements and complete the reported statements in the past tense.

1. **Carol Perkins, police officer:** "We will investigate the reports. Please wait. The sheriff may ask you for a statement."

   The police officer told the witnesses that _they would investigate the reports._

   She asked them _____ because _____

   _____

2. **Tony Shaw, truck driver:** "I'm sure I saw a UFO."

   The witness said _____

3. **Julie Pacino, administrative assistant:** "I don't believe in UFOs, but I've never seen anything like it before."

   The woman said _____

   but she admitted that _____

4. **David Bane, farmer:** "The object stopped right over my house, and then it disappeared."

   The farmer claimed that _____

   _____

5. **Jane and Kevin Baxter, retired:** "We followed it for fifty miles in our car. We took some photos."

   The couple reported that _____

   and said that _____

6. **Peter Cowden, elementary school student:** "What's a UFO? Is it something like a jet?"

   A boy asked _____ He also wanted to know

   _____

Completing Sentences with *Tell, Say,* and *Ask*

Choose a beginning for each sentence by placing a check (✓) in the appropriate column. In some cases, two answers may be correct.

SHE TOLD	SHE SAID	SHE ASKED	
✓		✓	1. ـــــــ her friends to come.
			2. ـــــــ she'd be on time.
			3. ـــــــ us if we'd be there.
			4. ـــــــ that she was working.
			5. ـــــــ us that she'd be late.
			6. ـــــــ us to be there at six.
			7. ـــــــ when we'd arrive.
			8. ـــــــ that the meeting should start on time.

MEANING AND USE

4) Changing Pronouns and Adverbs in Quoted Speech

Write the reported speech as quoted speech. Change the pronouns, verb forms, and adverbs as necessary.

1. He said he'd met me the previous week.

   "I met you last week." _____

2. He said he'd met me before.

   _____

3. He said he was angry at his brother.

   _____

4. He said he would help me the next day.

   _____

5. He said I looked like my mother.

   _____

6. He said he was arriving the following Monday.

   _____

Rewrite the quoted speech as reported speech. Use the simple past. Use one of the verbs in the box with a *that* clause in each sentence.

admitted	mentioned	pointed out	reminded
complained	announced	promised	shouted

1. "By the way, we're thinking about having a party on Friday." (David)

   David mentioned that they were thinking about having a party

   on Friday.

2. "The electricity will be turned off in your area between 10:00 and 11:00 A.M. tomorrow." (The electric company)

   _____

   _____

3. "Lee, remember that it can get cold in the mountains." (Mom)

   _____

   _____

4. "I didn't have time to finish the report." (Bill)

   _____

   _____

5. "Someone's hurt! I need a doctor!" (A man)

   _____

   _____

6. "The room is dirty, and there aren't any towels." (The hotel guest)

   _____

   _____

7. "I'll take a look at your car as soon as possible." (The mechanic)

   _____

   _____

8. "There are several misspelled words in your paper." (The professor)

   _____

   _____

6 Completing Statements with Reporting Verbs

Choose one or two correct words or phrases to complete each sentence.

1. My father _____ me he would pay for me to go to college.

   (a.) promised

   b. convinced

   (c.) told

2. My uncle _____ to me that his son would inherit his property.

   a. said

   b. informed

   c. explained

3. The man _____ that the game had been canceled.

   a. notified

   b. informed

   c. announced

4. Amy's brothers _____ her that her parents were angry at her.

   a. persuaded

   b. convinced

   c. said

5. Mary _____ that she wasn't feeling well.

   a. replied

   b. told

   c. reminded

6. The doctors _____ me that my son would not feel any pain.

   a. complained

   b. assured

   c. notified

7. My sister _____ that she was going to have a baby.

   a. announced

   b. informed

   c. indicated

8. My mother _____ that she wasn't happy.

   a. admitted

   b. complained

   c. told

COMBINING FORM, MEANING, AND USE

7 ▸ Thinking About Meaning and Use

Complete this story by writing one appropriate word in each blank. In some cases, more than one answer is possible.

My mother believes in ghosts. A few years ago, she __told__ me that my

grandmother, who died before I was born, visits her regularly before she goes to sleep.

I asked her _____ my grandmother spoke to her. "Of course she does," she

answered, adding that my grandmother _____ given her advice throughout

her adult life. I asked my mother why she _____ told me this before. "I

didn't think you _____ believe me," she answered.

When I _____ my father what my mother had _____, he

_____ that my grandmother always gave good advice. It was my

grandmother who _____ my mother not to stay in Los Angeles. She begged

my parents _____ sell their house there, and so they did—just before a

large earthquake hit the area.

8 ▸ Writing

Follow the steps below to write a paragraph about a story or conversation.

1. Think about a story from a book, TV, or a movie; or a conversation from real life or your imagination, in which someone said something funny, or two people became angry at each other.

2. Write five things that people actually said in the story or conversation. Use quoted speech.

3. On a separate sheet of paper, write a one-paragraph description of the story or the conversation. Use reported speech with *that, if/whether* and *wh-* clauses or infinitives when possible. Use a variety of reporting verbs.

> I rented a video with Tom Cruise and Jack Nicholson
>
> called <u>A Few Good Men</u>. In the movie Cruise got very angry
>
> and told Nicholson that he wanted the truth. Nicholson
>
> looked at him and shouted . . . .

Chapters 17–18

A. Complete these sentences with one correct word or phrase.

1. He recognized her face. He was sure that they ＿＿ before.
   a. had met   **b.** meet   **c.** met

2. My parents always told ＿＿ education was important.
   a. me that   **b.** that   **c.** whether

3. I didn't know ＿＿ we were going to do.
   a. that   **b.** what   **c.** whether

4. I was wondering ＿＿ I could observe your class.
   a. if   **b.** that   **c.** what

5. The bank notified ＿＿ they would be changing their interest rate.
   a. us   **b.** us that   **c.** that

6. The guide explained ＿＿ there were ruins under the church.
   a. that   **b.** us   **c.** us that

7. I thought you ＿＿ never get here.
   a. will   **b.** won't   **c.** would

8. My friend said ＿＿ there were ghosts in the graveyard.
   a. me that   **b.** me   **c.** that

B. Find and correct one error in each of the following sentences.

9. My father asked me what was the reason for my bad grades.

10. My mother thinks what the newspapers tell the truth.

11. I do not know how many students are there in my class.

12. Some people don't care that they work or not.

13. The situation is so bad that people do not know when will they be able to go home.

14. Some people say that that are not enough jobs for students.

15. You have to know what are your priorities.

16. You don't realize how difficult is the work.

C. Rewrite the following questions, beginning with the words given.
Use noun clauses.

17. What time is it?

    Do you know _____

18. Is it time to go?

    Tell me _____

19. Does he like it?

    I wonder _____

20. When does it start?

    Do you know _____

21. Where did Ben go?

    Does anybody know _____

22. Did they find anything?

    Do you know _____

23. What did she do?

    I don't understand _____

D. Report what the real estate agent said to the young couple. Choose one of the
verbs in parentheses and rewrite the quoted speech as reported speech.

24. "I think you should look at this house." (recommend, admit)

    _____

25. "You want a view of the ocean, remember?" (remind, warn)

    _____

26. "The house needs a little work." (advise, admit)

    _____

27. "You'll have to decide fast." (admit, warn)

    _____

28. "By the way, the house has a garage." (mention, recommend)

    _____

29. "The price is low because the owners want to move." (advise, explain)

    _____

30. "You really must go and see it." (advise, remind)

    _____

Answer Key

Chapter 1 The Present

Exercise 1 (p. 1)

1. line 4:   eats
   line 5:   runs out
   line 10: goes
   line 16: knows
   line 17: takes
   line 21: studies
   line 21: takes
   line 22: hires
   line 23: leaves
   line 25: does . . . want
   line 27: knows
   line 29: don't get
   line 31: work
   line 32: come
   line 37: realize
   line 41: changes

2. line 11: 's getting
   line 34: are becoming
   line 37: are spending
   line 39: (are) playing
   line 40: (are) sleeping

3. line 23:   She never leaves them in the hands of a babysitter even if she does sometimes want to have an afternoon for herself.
   b

Exercise 2 (p. 2)

2. Does his sister Fumie study in sixth grade?
3. How many days does she go to juku?
4. Does their mother study with her children?
5. Does she teach them herself?
6. Why don't Japanese fathers get involved in their children's education?
7. When do they usually come home?
8. What do more Japanese realize today?

Exercise 3 (p. 3)

2. are filling up
3. 're looking
4. 're walking
5. 's . . . doing
6. Is . . . arguing
7. isn't arguing
8. 's . . . wishing
9. are taking off
10. is . . . getting started
11. is taking
12. is doing
13. is making
14. are raising
15. is starting

Exercise 4 (p. 4)

2. PC
3. PC
4. SP
5. SP
6. SP

2.
b. 1
c. 6
d. 3
e. 4
f. 2

Exercise 5 (p. 5)

2. A
3. S
4. A
5. A
6. S
7. S
8. S

Exercise 6 (p. 5)

2. b   3. a   4. b   5. c   6. c   7. b   8. a

Exercise 7 (p. 7)

            'm writing
I ~~write~~ this letter because I have a serious problem. I

                     I don't believe
work in a stressful job, but ~~I'm not believing~~ it's worse

than what most people face at work. My problem is that

I cry   go   know
~~I'm crying~~ too easily when things ~~goes~~ wrong. I ~~knowing~~ I

have to get stronger. I don't deal well with

disappointment or criticism. It's ~~being~~ very embarrassing.

            is becoming
In fact, the situation ~~becomes~~ more and more difficult.

What advice do you have for me?

                         Cry Baby in Dallas

Dear Cry Baby:

                  get
Most of us ~~gets~~ upset when others criticize us. But

                You don't appear
you are ~~being~~ right: ~~You're not appearing~~ professional

when you cry at work. Sometimes we need~~s~~ to cry, but

tears don't belong~~s~~ on the job. If you think you're going

to cry, go to the restroom and do it there. And please, see

a therapist to help you with your emotions.

Exercise 8 (p. 7)
Answers will vary.

136   Answer Key

Chapter 2 The Past

Exercise 1 (p. 8)

1. line 2: traveled   line 11: opposed, hoped
   line 3: met   line 12: threatened
   line 5: expressed   line 13: approached
   line 7: returned   line 14: earned
   line 9: began   line 17: made
2. line 9: was becoming
   line 10: were killing
   line 15: was sleeping
3. line 9: . . . when Fossey began her research
   line 15: . . . while she was sleeping at her campsite

Exercise 2 (p. 9)

Conversation 1

Hector: I overslept. I didn't wake up until 8:30.

Rosa: Did your boss see you?

Hector: She saw me when I came in.

Rosa: Did she say anything to you?

Hector: She didn't say anything, but she gave me a dirty look.

Conversation 2

Eva: Sorry. Were you trying to sleep?

Elena: No. I wasn't sleeping. I was reading.

Eva: Well, first Sasha and I were watching a great TV program.

Elena: Is that why you were laughing so hard?

Eva: For part of the time. Later, we were laughing because we were looking at some old pictures of you!

Exercise 3 (p. 10)

A. 2. when you ate in that fancy restaurant?
    3. after I gave you my number?
    4. when you were growing up?
    5. before you had a car?
    6. while you were unemployed?

B. b. 3   c. 2   d. 6   e. 1   f. 5

C. a. 4, 6   b. 2, 3, 5

Exercise 4 (p. 11)

2. were waiting for   11. was shaking
3. heard   12. introducing
4. looked   13. chatted
5. didn't see   14. were talking
6. knew   15. realized
7. saw   16. was getting
8. was standing   17. said
9. was washing
10. called

Exercise 5 (p. 11)

A. 2. a   3. a   4. b   5. b   6. b

B. 2. c   3. a, b, c   4. a, b   5. c, e   6. a, b

Exercise 6 (p. 12)

2. b, c   3. a, b   4. c   5. b   6. a, c

Exercise 7 (p. 13)

~~I'm having~~ *I have* so many wonderful memories of my childhood. ~~While~~ *When* I was three years old, my family moved to Costa Rica. For the first few years, we lived in a small apartment. Then, when ~~it's~~ *it was* time for my brother and me to start school, my parents ~~were buying~~ *bought* our first house. For the first time, I had my own room and didn't ~~had~~ *have* to share with my sister. I ~~was loving~~ *loved* that room! My mother ~~was liking~~ *liked* to sew, and she made a beautiful bedspread and matching curtains.

We didn't have a lot of free time during the week, but weekends were always ~~being~~ a lot of fun. On Saturdays, we always ~~play~~ *played* games together. Sunday was my favorite day because we almost always went to the beach. We ~~were packing~~ *packed* a big lunch, and Dad barbecue*d* hamburgers or chicken. We kids were ~~being~~ sleepy after we ~~were eating~~ *ate*, so we spread blankets under a big tree and ~~take~~ *took* naps.

Exercise 8 (p. 14)

Answers will vary.

Chapter 3 Future Forms

Exercise 1 (p. 15)

1. line 5: are going to be   line 31: will understand
   line 8: will be growing   line 32: will invent
   line 10: (will be) transplanting   line 34: will talk
   line 14: will get   line 40: will be
   line 15: won't be traveling   line 41: will be
   line 21: will be   line 44: will die
   line 24: 'll be flying   line 46: will . . . be like
   line 26: will come   line 49: is going out of business
   line 27: (will) pick . . . up   line 53: 'll be doing
2. line 43: When that happens . . .
3. b

Exercise 2 (p. 16)

2. Jane will be teaching her nieces how to bowl.
3. David will be shopping with his grandmother.
4. Takeshi will be helping Jessica.
5. Celia will be catching up on her homework.
6. Rachel will be working.

Exercise 3 (p. 16)

2. It begins
3. When does it end?
4. It ends
5. When do the boat races start?
6. They start
7. How long do they/the boat races last?
8. They last
9. How much does the celebration cost?
10. It costs

Exercise 4 (p. 17)

2. b, c　　3. b　　4. a, b, c　　5. a　　6. a, b, c

Exercise 5 (p. 17)

2. Before she goes food shopping, she's going to write down the grocery list./She's going to write down the grocery list before she goes food shopping.
3. After she bakes the turkey for six hours at 375°, she's going to take it out of the oven./She's going to take the turkey out of the oven after she bakes it for six hours at 375°.
4. As soon as she polishes the silver, she's going to set the table./She's going to set the table as soon as she polishes the silver.
5. She's going to wait to add the dressing until she prepares all the ingredients for the salad./Until she prepares all the ingredients for the salad, she's going to wait to add the dressing.
6. She's going to wash the kitchen floor after she sweeps it./After she sweeps the kitchen floor, she's going to wash it.

Exercise 6 (p. 18)

(Any combination of the following forms is acceptable.)

　　b.　**Hiro:** What are you going to do next Saturday?
　　　Koji: Yuko and I are spending the day at the beach.
2. a.　**Ben:** When are you going to finish final exams?
　　　Kevin: I'm finishing next week.
　　b.　**Ben:** When are you finishing final exams?
　　　Kevin: I'm going to finish next week.
3. a. **David:** How are you celebrating your birthday this year?
　　　Kate: My parents are going to throw me a big party.
　　b. **David:** How are you going to celebrate your birthday this year?
　　　Kate: My parents are throwing me a big party.

4. a. **Emily:** What are you going to do after graduation?
　　　Tony: I'm leaving on a trip to Mexico.
　　b. **Emily:** What are you doing after graduation?
　　　Tony: I'm going to leave on a trip to Mexico.

Exercise 7 (p. 19)

People predict that genetic engineering ~~has~~ *will have* a major effect on our food supply in the future. Genetically engineered fruits, vegetables, and animals will help increase the food supply. For example, it is possible that people ~~are growing~~ *will grow* tropical fruits such as bananas, coconuts, and pineapples in colder climates such as Canada or Russia. Foods on supermarket shelves are going *to* taste better and last longer. Since these foods won't spoil as quickly, they ~~are being~~ *will be* abundant and cheap.

These new foods *are* also going to be better for you. Scientists *will* manipulate the DNA of many foods to make them more nutritious and allergy-free. Potatoes ~~will be having~~ *will have* a special gene so that when people make French fries, they ~~aren't soaking~~ *won't soak* up as much oil. And there may even be special fruits and vegetables that act like vaccines. So instead of getting a shot to prevent disease, people ~~are eating~~ *will eat* an apple or a carrot!

Exercise 8 (p. 19)

Answers will vary.

See page 153 for Key to Review: Chapter 1-3.

Chapter 4 The Present Perfect

Exercise 1 (p. 22)

1. line 12: have gone　　line 21: have performed
　 line 16: has maintained　line 23: has succeeded
　 line 17: have returned　　line 27: have found

Exercise 2 (p. 23)

2. 've been　　　　7. haven't eaten
3. has been　　　　8. Have you seen
4. have you ordered　9. 've eaten
5. has come　　　　10. 've never had
6. haven't ordered　11. 've paid

12. 've had
13. 've raised
14. Have you decided
15. Have you heard
16. has prepared

Exercise 3 (p. 24)

A.
2. Eighty-nine percent have told a white lie.
3. Sixty-seven percent have called in sick to work when they were healthy.
4. Sixty percent have parked illegally.
5. Fifty-seven percent have cheated on an exam.
6. Forty-three percent have written a personal E-mail at work.
7. Thirty-eight percent have made a long-distance phone call at work.
8. Nineteen percent have cut into a line.

B.
2. Q: Have you ever told a white lie?
   A: (Answers will vary.)
3. Q: Have you ever called in sick to work when you were healthy?
   A: (Answers will vary.)
4. Q: Have you ever parked illegally?
   A: (Answers will vary.)
5. Q: Have you ever cheated on an exam?
   A: (Answers will vary.)
6. Q: Have you ever written a personal e-mail at work?
   A: (Answers will vary.)
7. Q: Have you ever made a long-distance phone call at work?
   A: (Answers will vary.)
8. Q: Have you ever cut into a line?
   A: (Answers will vary.)

Exercise 4 (p. 25)

2. since
3. recently/lately
4. lately/recently
5. just
6. for
7. since
8. for

Exercise 5 (p. 26)

2. Gina: Have you chosen a hotel in Buenos Aires yet?
   Steve: Yes, I chose the Olympic.
3. Gina: Have you paid the room deposit yet?
   Steve: No, I haven't. I will tomorrow.
4. Steve: Have you renewed our passports?
   Gina: Yes, I have. I did it on Wednesday.
5. Steve: Have you reserved a rental car?
   Gina: No, I haven't. I've been too busy.

Exercise 6 (p. 27)

2. b 3. a 4. a 5. a 6. b 7. b 8. a 9. a 10. a

Exercise 7 (p. 28)

Answers will vary.

Chapter 5 The Present Perfect Continuous

Exercise 1 (p. 29)

1. line 3: has . . . been working on
   line 6: 's been working
   line 8: has been making
   line 16: has been frightening

2. line 3: has . . . been working on
   line 6: 's been working
   line 8: has been making
   line 16: has been frightening

Exercise 2 (p. 30)

Conversation 1
2. 've been calling
3. has been trying
4. 've been asking

Conversation 2
1. Has she been avoiding
2. 's been working
3. 's been getting
4. hasn't been doing
5. 's been taking

Conversation 3
1. have you been planning
2. 've been preparing
3. have been making
4. 've been watching
5. 've been improving
6. 've been skating

Exercise 3 (p. 31)

2. He's been going to parties lately, and he hasn't been studying enough.
3. He's just been talking to his grandmother, and she hasn't been feeling well.
4. She hasn't been sleeping well lately because she's been having nightmares.
5. They haven't been spending time with friends recently because they've been painting their house.
6. She hasn't been going straight home after work because she's been going to the hospital to visit her uncle.

Exercise 4 (p. 32)

2. a 3. a 4. a 5. b 6. a 7. b 8. a

Exercise 5 (p. 32)

Conversation 1
2. 've been thinking
3. haven't spoken
4. called
5. 's been traveling
6. (has) promised

Conversation 2
1. Have you read
2. haven't seen
3. has been making
4 knew
5. 's worked
6. haven't seen
7. Has she been working
8. 's been taking
9. loved

Exercise 6 (p. 33)

2. b, c   5. a, c
3. a, b   6. a, c
4. c, d

Exercise 7 (p. 34)

Soccer is the most popular international team sport. Historians believe that people ~~has~~ *have* been playing soccer since the year 217 A.D., when the first game ~~has been~~ *was* part of a victory celebration in England. Soccer became popular in Europe over the centuries, and eventually it spread throughout most of the world. In the United States, soccer has always been ~~being~~ secondary to American football. Recently, however, soccer has ∧*been* growing in popularity.

In 1904, several nations ~~have~~ formed the International Federation of Football (FIFA), which has been regulating international competition ~~since~~ *for* over a century. Since 1930, the World Cup ~~have~~ *has* been bringing countries together. And although women ~~weren't~~ *haven't been* playing soccer for as long as men have, an important international event, the Women's World Cup, has been ~~taken~~ *taking* place every four years since 1991.

Exercise 8 (p. 35)

Answers will vary.

Chapter 6 The Past Perfect and the Past Perfect Continuous

Exercise 1 (p. 36)

1. line 2: had been thinking
   line 10: had been going
2. line 3: 'd . . . had   line 11: had offered
   line 4: hadn't been   line 12: hadn't . . . discussed
   line 5: had known   line 14: had . . . wanted
   line 6: had . . . argued   line 16: had . . . known
   line 6: had become   line 17: had . . . loved
3. *a* is incorrect. The past perfect uses only one auxiliary.
   b and *c* are correct.

Exercise 2 (p. 37)

2. he had never washed his own dishes.
3. he had never made his own bed.
4. he had never done his own laundry.

Exercise 3 (p. 37)

2. When Chris and Emily arrived, the group had been pulling weeds for twenty-five minutes.
3. When Sasha came, the group had been washing the benches for five minutes.
4. When Jane got there, the group had been painting the benches for half an hour thirty minutes.
5. When Mr. and Mrs. Rivera came, the group had been cleaning the playground for twenty minutes.
6. When Rick arrived, the group had been raking leaves for fifteen minutes.

Exercise 4 (p. 38)

2. Picasso had drawn his first picture before he spoke his first word. OR Before he spoke his first word, Picasso had drawn his first picture.
3. Picasso had lived in Málaga until he entered the Royal Academy in Madrid. OR Until he entered the Royal Academy in Madrid, Picasso had lived in Málaga.
4. Picasso had produced more than 1,000 works of art by the time he was 23 years old. OR By the time he was 23 years old, Picasso had produced more than 1,000 works of art.
5. Picasso became well-known after he had moved to Paris. OR After Picasso had moved to Paris, he became well-known.
6. The history of art changed forever after Picasso painted *Les Demoisels d' Avignon*. OR After Picasso painted *Les Demoisels d' Avignon*, the history of art changed forever.
7. Picasso painted his anti-war painting *Guernica* after the Nazis bombed Guernica, Spain. OR After the Nazis bombed Guernica, Spain, Picasso painted his anti-war painting *Guernica*.
8. Picasso had lived in Paris for many years when he moved to southern France. OR When he moved to southern France, Picasso had lived in Paris for many years.
9. Jacqueline Roque had been Picasso's companion for seven years before they got married. OR Before they got married, Jacqueline Roque had been Picasso's companion for seven years.
10. Picasso had lived in Mougins for almost 20 years before he died. OR Before he died, Picasso had lived in Mougins for almost 20 years.

Exercise 5 (p. 40)

B. 2. The group hadn't cut the grass yet, but they had already pulled weeds.
3. The group hadn't raked leaves yet, but they had already picked up the trash.
4. The group hadn't planted flowers yet, but they had already trimmed the trees.
5. The group hadn't emptied the trash cans yet, but they had planted flowers.

Exercise 6 (p. 41)

2. I bought a new car because my old one had been acting up.
3. My eyes were aching although I'd taken a nap after lunch.
4. My eyes were aching because I'd been studying very hard.
5. My eyes were aching because I'd been working at the computer for hours.
6. My eyes were aching because I'd left my glasses at home.
7. My teacher loved my report although I hadn't worked very hard on it.
8. My grades were terrible although I'd been studying very hard.
9. My grades were terrible because I hadn't been taking good class notes lately.
10. I'd never bought a new car although my parents had always promised to help with the payments.
11. I'd never bought a new car because I'd never had enough money.
12. I got a low grade on my report because I hadn't worked very hard on it.

Exercise 7 (p. 42)

2. b, d   4. b, d   6. b, c
3. b, c   5. a, c

Exercise 8 (p. 42)

Answers will vary.

See page 153 for Key to Review: Chapters 4-6.

Chapter 7 Modals of Possibility

Exercise 1 (p. 46)

1. line 4: could   line 12: could
    line 5: 's got to   line 13: should
    line 9: could   line 15: may not
    line 11: might   line 16: ought to
2. a, c

Exercise 2 (p. 47)

2. Correct
3. Incorrect

        may not
    I ~~mayn't~~ be in class tomorrow.
4. Correct
5. Incorrect

    Could
    ~~Should~~ the accused man be innocent?
6. Incorrect

        can't
    This ~~hasn't got to~~ be right. It makes no sense.
7. Correct
8. Incorrect

    Steve must feel~~s~~ terrible about this.

Exercise 3 (p. 47)

Conversation 1

2. ought to be
3. he can't be
4. may be
5. we might miss
6. That has to be
7. could he be calling
8. He must be calling

Conversation 2

1. This can't be happening
2. we might be running out of
3. How could that be
4. has to be
5. could be
6. we should be
7. ought to be

Exercise 4 (p. 48)

a. 2, 3, 5
b. 1, 10
c. 4, 8, 9
d. 6, 7

Exercise 5 (p. 49)

2. should/ought to
3. could/might/may
4. must/'ve got to/have to
5. must/have got to/have to
6. should/ought to
7. should/ought to
8. should/must/'s got to/has to
9. should/ought to/must
10. could/might/may

Exercise 6 (p. 50)

2. It should be/ought to be cooler tonight.
3. It could/may/might rain tomorrow.
4. It could/may/might be warmer on Thursday.
5. It won't snow on Saturday.
6. The temperature will drop tomorrow.

Exercise 7 (p. 50)

2. D
   She's got to be upset.
3. D
   I might be late tonight.
4. S
5. D
   It might/may rain any minute.
6. S
7. S

8. D
   It ought to be great.
9. D
   This must/has got to be the place.
10. S

Exercise 8 (p. 52)

Hi, Dr. Carter. I'm writing to tell you that I probably
~~mightn't~~ *won't* be in class next week. My grandfather may

need~~s~~ an operation, and my parents want me to come

home to be with the family. No one has told me yet what

kind of surgery Grandpa needs, but it ~~should~~ *must/has to/has got to* be serious.

Otherwise, my family wouldn't be suggesting that I make

the long trip home. ~~You'll~~ *You* may find this a bit unusual, but

I'm very close to my grandfather. I know this absence

could ~~to~~ put my grade in danger, but I'll work very hard

so that I don't fall behind.

You ~~mayn't~~ *may not* be very happy about this, but I need to

ask a special favor. Do you think you might ~~being~~ *be* able to

E-mail me next week's assignments? That way, I ~~maybe~~ *may be*

able to do some of them while I'm away. I'm not sure, but

I should ~~am~~ *be* getting back to Los Angeles by April 1.

Thank you very much.

Matt Kennedy

Exercise 9 (p. 52)

Answers will vary.

Chapter 8 Past Modals

Exercise 1 (p. 53)

1. line 7: couldn't have been   line 14: could have pulled
   line 9: may have been   line 14: would have worn down
   line 10: couldn't have used   line 15: would have . . . polished
   line 12: must have provided
2. a, b

Exercise 2 (p. 54)

2. I could have picked you up at the airport last weekend.
3. The students might not have understood everything on yesterday's test.

4. David must have been at the office yesterday afternoon.
5. We could have gone to the mountains last summer.
6. There must have been a lot of traffic this morning.
7. The company might have solved its financial problems last year.
8. You shouldn't have stayed up late last night.

Exercise 3 (p. 54)

Conversation 1

2. could have happened
3. might not have received
4. must have gone

Conversation 2

1. might have caught
2. should have gotten
3. shouldn't have taken
4. had to have been laughing

Exercise 4 (p. 55)

1. b. She might have/may have/could have secretly returned to the United States.
   c. She must have/had to have/'s got to have run out of fuel and crashed.
2. a. The builders must have/had to have/have got to have traveled over land and sea to bring the stones for the monument.
   b. The building of the monument couldn't have/can't have started before 3000 B.C.
   c. The structure might have/could have/may have been a temple.

Exercise 5 (p. 56)

2. They couldn't have finished the homework. They may have started the homework.
3. They can't have gotten to Washington in less than an hour. They might have gotten there in less than three hours.
4. Rick couldn't have robbed the bank. Someone else must have robbed the bank.
5. They can't have won a million dollars. They must have received an advertisement.
6. The President can't have called you yesterday. It must have been a joke.
7. Kim can't have cooked a three-course meal by herself. Her mother must have helped.
8. Lee couldn't have completed the race in under an hour. He might have completed it in an hour and a half.

Exercise 6 (p. 57)

Answers will vary. Some examples are:
2. They should have/ought to have removed their identification badges during the robbery.
3. They shouldn't have/ought not to have gone back to work after committing the crime.
4. They should have realized the police would find them.

Exercise 7 (p. 57)

2. I shouldn't have/ought not to have gotten married so young
3. I should have/ought to have taken better care of my teeth
4. I should have/ought to have gone to college
5. I should have/ought to have exercised more
6. I shouldn't have/ought not to have worked so hard
7. I should have/ought to have learned to control my temper
8. I shouldn't have/ought not to have skipped my medical checkups.

Exercise 8 (p. 58)

2. a, d   4. a, d   6. c, d   8. a, d
3. b, d   5. b, c   7. b, d

Exercise 9 (p. 59)

Answers will vary.

See page 158 for Key to Review Chapters 7-8.

Chapter 9 Passive Sentences (Part I)

Exercise 1 (p. 63)

1. line 5: is removed
   line 6: are . . . shut off
   line 8: is removed

2. line 1: were surprised
   line 2: was discovered
   line 9: was . . . proven
   line 11: were placed
   line 11: (were) put
   line 12: were covered
   line 13: were plugged
   line 13: were told
   line 18: were visited

3. line 4: are being given
   line 14: were being observed

Exercise 2 (p. 64)

A. 2. is considered
   3. is filled
   4. are made up
   5. are entertained
   6. are thrown
   7. are caught
   8. are enjoyed

B.   Last week, Mardi Gras, or Fat Tuesday, *was celebrated* in many cities around the world, but Mardi Gras in New Orleans, Louisiana, *was considered* by many to be the most spectacular. During the week before Fat Tuesday, the French Quarter of New Orleans *was filled* with long, winding parades. These parades *were made up* of magnificent floats and marching bands. Spectators *were entertained* by a variety of performers. Plastic bead necklaces and a variety of toys *were thrown* from the floats, and these "treasures" *were caught* by the spectators lining the parade route. The parades *were enjoyed* by thousands of people.

Exercise 3 (p. 64)

A. 2. is being blamed
   3. are being turned
   4. are being trapped
   5. are being created
   6. are being blocked
   7. are being clogged
   8. is being threatened

B. The beautiful water hyacinth *was being blamed* for causing serious ecological damage. Bays *were being turned* into muddy swamps. As a result, boats *were being trapped*, and breeding grounds for mosquitoes *were being created*.
    The water hyacinth had never grown in Victoria until about 15 years ago, and no one knows how it got there. Because of the plant's floating leaves, harbors *were being blocked*. The pipes at a power station *were being clogged*. Fishing *was being threatened* as well.

Exercise 4 (p. 65)

2. The study was completed last month.
3. The children didn't eat breakfast this morning.
4. The house is cleaned by the housekeeper once a week./The house was cleaned by the housekeeper once a week.
5. The accident occurred last Sunday.
6. Our house was destroyed by the flood a year ago.
7. Many tourists visit our city in the summer./Many tourists visited our city in the summer.
8. The employees are allowed to leave early on Fridays./The employees were allowed to leave early on Fridays.

Exercise 5 (p. 66)

A.

	HAS ONLY AN ACTIVE FORM	HAS A PASSIVE FORM
1. The city recently built a new parking garage.		✓
2. Parking was becoming a serious problem.	✓	
3. Cars were filling up the parking lots by 11 A.M.		✓
4. Construction of the garage cost a million dollars.	✓	
5. The city is also putting in a park near the garage.		✓
6. The park has a rose garden.	✓	
7. A landscaping company is planting the rose bushes.		✓
8. Many people now visit the park during lunch hour.		✓
9. A photo of the park appeared in today's newspaper.	✓	
10. The newspaper also published an article about the park.		✓
11. The company grows all kinds of roses.		✓
12. Workers downtown appreciate the improvements.		✓

B.
2. X
3. The parking lots were being filled up by cars by 11 A.M.
4. X
5. A park is being put in near the garage by the city.
6. X
7. All kinds of roses are grown by the company.
8. The park is now visited by many people during lunch hour.
9. X
10. An article about the park was also published by the newspaper.
11. The rose bushes are being planted by a landscaping company.
12. The improvements are appreciated by workers downtown.

Exercise 6 (p. 67)

2. are brought
3. chose
4. is chosen
5. kill
6. fell
7. was watched
8. watched
9. was killed
10. brings
11. is watched
12. were killed
13. is sung
14. sang
15. played
16. is played

Exercise 7 (p. 68)

2. a. T
   b. F
   c. F
3. a. ?
   b. F
   c. F
4. a. F
   b. T
   c. ?
5. a. F
   b. T
   c. T
6. a. T
   b. F
   c. ?

Exercise 8 (p. 69)

Animal groups are ~~classifying~~ classified according to their basic structure. For billions of years, animals have kept certain features that are ~~use~~ used to identify them. For example, all mammals have backbones and are warm-blooded, features that are also seen in birds.

The whale is a special case. Originally, all mammals ~~were~~ lived on land. Their bodies were ~~keeping~~ kept warm by a covering of hair, and they ~~were~~ walked on four legs. They breathed air through nostrils into their lungs. A whale looks so different that it is often mistaken for a fish. A closer look shows that it is a mammal that has adapted to living in water. It is covered with a thick coat of fat, or blubber. Thanks to a whale's blubber, the warmth ~~was~~ is retained in the body and the animal can tolerate very low temperatures.

Exercise 9 (p. 70)

Answers will vary.

Chapter 10 Passive Sentences (Part II)

Exercise 1 (p. 71)

1. Passive forms
   line 4: will be disconnected
   line 5: is not made
   line 6: can be made
   line 7: will be charged
   line 8: is made
   line 8: (is) not kept
   line 8: may be shut off
   line 9: has . . . been made

2a. line 9: has already been made
   b. line 4: will be disconnected
      line 7: will be charged
   c. line 6: can be made
      line 8: may be shut off

Exercise 2 (p. 72)

2. will not be tolerated
3. can't be repaired
4. has got to be done (about the noise)
5. need to be rewritten
6. might not be published
7. must be found and arrested
8. will be notified (if your nomination is accepted)
9. might be given a ticket
10. should not be penalized (for this)
11. The room will be painted tomorrow.
12. You might be stopped if you try to go in without a ticket.

Exercise 3 (p. 73)

2. An energy company has been caught in a scandal.
3. A fireman has been honored with medals.
4. The captives have been freed in a UN rescue operation.
5. A $4.4 million budget has been approved.
6. A national wildlife reserve has been endangered by a fire.
7. A drug company has been fined in a lawsuit.
8. The President has been asked to sign an education bill.
9. A new cancer drug has been approved by the government.
10. Baseball has been added to Olympic sports.
11. $3.5 million has been raised for the Brazilian rainforest.
12. A swimmer in Florida has been bitten by a shark.

Exercise 4 (p. 74)

3. The fish is caught and frozen immediately ~~by the fishermen~~ to maintain freshness.
5. The woman was arrested ~~by the police~~ and taken into custody.
7. Because of the holiday, no mail will be delivered ~~by the letter carrier~~ on Thursday.
8. I think my watch has been stolen ~~by a thief~~.
10. The pilot was given clearance for takeoff ~~by the control tower~~.

Exercise 5 (p. 74)

2. c   3. e   4. f   5. d   6. b

Exercise 6 (p. 75)

                                          been
The mapping of the human genetic code has ʌ called
the most important scientific advance of our time. It will
transform
~~be transformed~~ medicine beyond recognition. New
             be developed
drugs will ~~develop~~ for previously untreatable diseases,
             be
and ways will ʌ found to replace or repair faulty genes.

Treatments will be matched to an individual's genetic

make-up and doctors will be able to predict the future of
their patients with much greater certainty.
                        disappear
      Some cancers will ~~be disappeared~~ completely, and
                                      be wiped
eventually, inherited diseases may ~~wipe~~ out by removing
faulty genes from the gene pool.

      However, many people believe that genetic
                        be used
information can ~~use~~ by insurance companies and
employers to discriminate against people on medical
grounds. In a speech praising the scientists, the
                                                          be
President warned that genetic information must never ʌ
used to segregate, discriminate against, or invade the
privacy of human beings.

Exercise 7 (p. 75)

Answers will vary.

Chapter 11 Contrasting Gerunds and Infinitives

Exercise 1 (p. 76)

1. line 3: to comfort   line 9:   to talk
   line 4: to go back   line 10: to be
   line 6: to leave   line 11: to change
   line 6: to obey   line 11: to get used to
2. line 6:   telling
   line 6:   refusing
   line 7:   crying
   line 13: hugging

Exercise 2 (p. 77)

2. Building a new library
3. to play with matches
4. Learning a new language
5. Parking in a bus zone
6. to surf the Internet
7. to go camping this weekend
8. to teach math

Exercise 3 (p. 77)

A. 2. learning   3. to go
B. 1. to understand   2. speaking   3. making
C. 1. to shop   2. going   3. clicking
D. 1. starting   2. giving   3. to get

Exercise 4 (p. 78)

2. S   4. D   6. S   8. D
3. S   5. D   7. S

Exercise 5 (p. 79)

2. a   4. a   6. a   8. c   10. c   12. a, b
3. b   5. c   7. b, c   9. b   11. a

Exercise 6 (p. 80)

2. to waste
3. running
4. standing
5. to go
6. shopping/to shop
7. to get
8. using/to use
9. to meet
10. running/to run
11. registering
12. cleaning

Exercise 7 (p. 80)

Answers will vary.

See page 154 for Key to Review Chapters 9-11.

Chapter 12 Indefinite and Definite Articles

Exercise 1 (p. 84)

1. line 4: a (comfortable) dorm
   line 5: a course
   line 7: a three-day weekend
2. line 3: the heart
   line 4: the Odéon
   line 6: the French language
   line 9: the theater
   line 9: the opera
   line 10: the evenings
   line 10: the Louvre
   line 11: the Musée d'Orsay
   line 11: the afternoons
3. (French) culture, (charming Breton) villages, (day) trips, visits

Exercise 2 (p. 85)

A.
2. a
3. an
4. a
5. a
6. a
7. an
8. a
9. an
10. an

B.
2. Ø sunscreen
3. a cooking stove
4. Ø fuel
5. Ø insect repellent
6. Ø dishes
7. a pocket knife
8. a flashlight
9. Ø soap
10. a sleeping bag

Exercise 3 (p. 85)

2. an
3. Ø
4. Ø
5. Ø
6. Ø
7. Ø
8. a
9. a
10. Ø
11. A
12. Ø
13. Ø
14. an
15. Ø
16. Ø
17. Ø
18. Ø

Exercise 4 (p. 86)

A.

Situation 1	Situation 2	Situation 3
2. b	1. c	1. c
	2. a	2. c
		3. c

B.

Situation 4	Situation 5
1. d	1. d
2. f	2. e
3. e	3. f

Exercise 5 (p. 87)

A.
2. the
3. an *or* the
4. the
5. the
6. the
7. the
8. the

B.
1. a
2. a
3. the
4. the
5. a
6. the
7. the

Exercise 6 (p. 88)

	GENERIC	SPECIFIC
2. <u>Orange-fleshed melons</u> are high in beta-carotene.	✓	
3. Most of <u>the melons</u> in our market come from Texas.		✓
4. <u>The cantaloupe</u> is actually a muskmelon.	✓	
5. I <u>bought</u> a cantaloupe on sale.		✓
6. <u>The cantaloupe</u> I had for breakfast was delicious.		✓

Exercise 7 (p. 88)

Everybody likes ~~a~~ *the* sun, especially when there are ~~the~~ blue skies above. But we now know that even on ~~the~~ *a* cloudy day in winter when you can't see ~~a~~ *the* sun, rays of the sun are constantly attacking our skin. In fact, daily ongoing sun protection is ~~an~~ *the* only way to stop wrinkles, because sun damage is the main reason we have wrinkles! So what you know about ~~a~~ sun protection today can literally save your skin.

During the summer, the sun's rays are strongest between 10 A.M. and 2 P.M. Clouds filter some of the rays, but not all, which is why you can still get burned on ∧ *an* overcast day. Different surfaces such as ~~a~~ water, sand, or snow can reflect the rays of the sun so ~~the~~ hats offer only partial protection.

Exercise 8 (p. 89)

Answers will vary.

Chapter 13 Relative Clauses with Subject Relative Pronouns

Exercise 1 (p. 90)

1. line 6: that contain just as much vitamin C as citrus fruits such as oranges or grapefruit
   line 14: who eat potatoes and whole-grain bread
   line 17: that satisfy your appetite
   line 19: that help fill you up
   line 26: who get more of their calories from fruits, grains, and vegetables
   line 29: which is often used to decorate dinner plates but usually remains uneaten
   line 34: that freshen your breath

2. line 6: vegetables
   line 14: People
   line 17: foods
   line 19: foods
   line 26: Europeans and Japanese
   line 29: Parsley
   line 34: ingredients

Exercise 2 (p. 91)

2. The lady who/that lives in the next apartment asked me to help her.
3. I inherited a Swiss watch that/which belonged to my father.
4. Do you see the girl who/that is wearing a long dress?
5. The cat that/which lives next door often visits me.
6. On the wall there are some photos that/which have faded in the sun.
7. Try out the chair that/which has a velvet back.
8. A warbler is a very small bird that sings beautiful songs.

Exercise 3 (p. 92)

2. My sister, who loves shopping, spends a lot of money on clothes.
3. Sarah wears shoes that/which make her look a lot taller.
4. The Clothes Rack, which has a store in our neighborhood, sells used clothing.
5. I bought a leather jacket that/which was on sale.
6. I'm the kind of person who/that prefers to wear casual clothes.
7. Bill decided to wear his gray suit, which was hanging in his closet.
8. I'm dating a woman who/that dresses like a fashion model.

Exercise 4 (p. 92)

2. We stayed with a cousin who lives nearby.
3. My cousin's children, who often visit my aunt, came with us.
4. My aunt lives in an apartment building which is a historical landmark.

5. Her room, which is on the ground floor, has a view of the gardens outside.
6. When we arrived we spoke to her neighbor, who has known her for a long time.
7. Aunt Luisa, who is almost blind, didn't recognize us at first.
8. But she got along well with my husband, who comes from her home state.
9. Even though she can no longer drive, she has an old Volkswagon that still looks brand new.
10. It's painted "sunshine yellow," which is a very bright color.

Exercise 5 (p. 93)

2. Lisa, who lives near you, might give you a ride.
3. We went to Bodega, which is a small town on the coast.
4. My friend Gina, who used to be a nurse, knows about fractures.
5. My computer, which cost me $1,500 a year ago, is on sale for $799.
6. I really enjoyed the book *Taxi*, which is about cab drivers in New York.
7. My cousin Amy, who got married in September, is moving to Alaska with her husband.
8. That house on Store Street, which was built in 1850, is for sale.

Exercise 6 (p. 94)

2. Chhiri was a remarkable mountaineer who reached the peak of Mt. Everest twice in fourteen days.
3. Chhiri, who came from a small village in the foothills of the Himalayas, first began to climb Everest when he was a porter for the more experienced Sherpas who guide foreigners up the mountain.
4. Chhiri, who ran an adventures firm that organized climbs for foreign teams, wanted greater respect for the Sherpas, who earn comparatively little money for their work.

Exercise 7 (p. 95)

Answers will vary.

Chapter 14 Relative Clauses with Object Relative Pronouns

Exercise 1 (p. 96)

1. line 10: biologists didn't foresee twenty-five years ago
   line 13: where the bears are found
   line 15: where bears have been for thousands of years
   line 18: that campers in national parks have learned
   line 19: you have
   line 19: that you leave around

2. line 10: threat
   line 13: areas
   line 14: places
   line 17: lessons
   line 18: garbage
   line 18: food

Exercise 2 (p. 97)

2. They've sold the house that you liked.
   They've sold the house you liked.
3. This is the dish that the chef recommends.
   This is the dish the chef recommends.
4. The woman that I met at the party gave me her number.
   The woman I met at the party gave me her number.
5. Would you like to try on the dress that you saw in the window?
   Would you like to try on the dress you saw in the window?
6. Something that I ate last night made me sick.
   Something I ate last night made me sick.
7. Would you like to see the car that I just bought?
   Would you like to see the car I just bought?
8. This is the wedding ring that my grandmother gave to me.
   This is the wedding ring my grandmother gave to me.

Exercise 3 (p. 98)

2. The movie I read about is on TV tonight.
3. Hiro's the guy I told you about.
4. Kate really likes the people she lives with.
5. The car belongs to the woman my husband works for.
6. Send the letter back to the person you got it from.
7. At last, here is the news we've been waiting for.
8. Is that the dog you're afraid of?

Exercise 4 (p. 98)

2. **Stefan:** Really? What about that girl you play basketball **with**, the one you told me **about?**
3. **Elena:** She's nice, but I don't like the people she hangs out **with**.
4. **Rosa:** My friend Carlos got the job I applied **for** at the bookstore.
5. **Yuko:** Really? Is Carlos the guy you used to work **with?**
6. **Rosa:** Yes. He's the one I introduced you **to** at the party.
7. **Mrs. Ruiz:** The house that the Smiths moved **into** isn't as nice as their old one.
8. **Mr. Ruiz:** Yes, but the golf club they belong **to** is right across the street.

Exercise 5 (p. 99)

2. Can you give me back the money that I lent you last week?
3. Mom, please read me the story that we read last night.
4. My aunt Rosa, whom I loved dearly, died last year.
5. The program that we saw on TV last night was really interesting.
6. My aunt brought me some tea, which I drank gratefully.
7. Our house, which my father had built himself, stood at the top of a hill.
8. We stopped at a campground that we had seen by the side of the river.

Exercise 6 (p. 100)

Answers will vary. Some examples are:

2. Winter is the season when it starts getting dark early.
3. I'll never forget the time when my brother spilled a can of paint on the floor.
4. In my house, the living room is the place where we watch TV.
5. One of my favorite cities is San Diego, which is sunny all year.
6. The kitchen is the place where people gather at parties.
7. 1945 is the year when World War II ended.
8. Sunday is the day when I sleep until eleven in the morning.
9. One of the best memories I have is the time when I got my drivers license.
10. New York City is the place where people like to go to the theater.

Exercise 7 (p. 101)

Venus and Serena Williams, ~~that~~ *who* took the tennis world by storm in the late 1990s, began their careers on the public courts of Compton, California. Compton was a long way from the clubs ~~that~~ *where* they would eventually play in the world's most prestigious tournaments. Tennis was not a popular sport for the neighborhood children, *who* were fans of the LA Lakers basketball team. When the sisters were teenagers, most of the people they practiced *with* were in their thirties and forties.

The girls soon began competitive play. But their father Richard, *who* has been their coach since they were young, kept them out of the high-pressure tournaments *where* ~~who~~ other girls played. According to the Women's Tennis Association rules, the number of tournaments a 16-year-old can play *in* is fourteen. At that age, Venus played in just four.

It wasn't only burnout that the girls' parents worried *about*. It was the pressures *that* competitive tennis can place on a family. "Tennis doesn't make a family strong. It makes a family weak," says their father, *who* ~~which~~ now oversees both girls' careers.

Exercise 8 (p. 102)

Answers will vary.

See page 154 for Review: Chapters 12-14.

Chapter 15 Real Conditionals, Unreal Conditionals, and Wishes

Exercise 1 (p. 105)

1. line 16: If I just stay here and try to relax, everything will be fine.
   line 30: If I tell them about it, they usually just say not to worry so much.
   line 34: If that is my problem, then tell me what to do.
2. line 25: If I could just leave, I would be able to do the things I need to do.
   lines 2–3: Often I wish I were a different person.

Exercise 2 (p. 106)

A.
2. will ('ll)
3. don't find
4. do
5. keeps
6. 'll go
7. won't have
8. will cook
9. come
10. 'll have

B.
2. had
3. saw
4. would buy
5. would be
6. told
7. would study
8. thought
9. lent
10. would buy

Exercise 3 (p. 107)

2. If the boy doesn't eat the ice cream, it will fall on the floor. Unless the boy eats the ice cream, it will fall on the floor.
3. If the water skier doesn't look out, he'll hit the swimmer. Unless the water skier looks out, he'll hit the swimmer.
4. If the woman doesn't pay attention, her purse will be stolen. Unless the woman pays attention, her purse will be stolen.

Exercise 4 (p. 108)

Answers will vary. Some examples are:
2. The staff won't work on Sunday unless **they get paid overtime.**
3. The plants will die unless **you water them.**
4. You won't get better unless **you take care of yourself.**
5. Don't call me unless **there's an emergency.**
6. My children won't eat vegetables unless **I put peanut butter on them.**
7. We'll run out of gas unless **we get some soon.**
8. She will get fired unless **she comes to work on time.**

Exercise 5 (p. 108)

2. a   3. a   4. b   5. b   6. a

Exercise 6 (p. 109)

2. Would you mind if I left early today?
3. Would it be OK if I came to see you in your office?
4. Would you mind if I was (were) late to class sometimes?
5. Would it bother you if I recorded the lectures?
6. Would it be a problem if I gave you the assignment on Monday?

Exercise 7 (p. 109)

Answers will vary. Some examples are:
2. If only I were **taller, I could play basketball.**
3. I wish my friends wouldn't **make fun of Yuki so much.**
4. I wish my teacher would **take a sick day once in a while.**
5. If only the weather were **warmer, we could hold class outside.**
6. I wish you wouldn't **snore so much at night.**

Exercise 8 (p. 110)

2. 'd have
3. had
4. have
5. 'll have
6. didn't have
7. had
8. don't have
9. 'll have
10. won't have

Exercise 9 (p. 110)

Answers will vary.

Chapter 16 Past Unreal Conditionals and Past Wishes

Exercise 1 (p. 111)

1. line 24:   might have been very different
   line 25:   would have walked
   line 29:   would have shot
   line 30:   wouldn't have had
   line 31:   wouldn't have bought
   line 32:   would have devastated
2. line 35: I just wish the police had caught those two men.

Exercise 2 (p. 112)

2. c   4. a   6. a   8. b
3. a   5. c   7. c

Exercise 3 (p. 112)

	HAD	WOULD
2. If Jake had been there, he'd have said something.		✓
3. If only we'd known!	✓	
4. You wouldn't have enjoyed the concert if you'd gone.	✓	
5. I'd have told you before, but I didn't know anything about it.		✓
6. If only you'd said something before now! We could have helped you.	✓	
7. Would he have been accepted if he'd gotten better grades?	✓	
8. They'd have told you by now if there were any openings.		✓

Exercise 4 (p. 113)

2. g   4. d   6. c   8. a
3. f   5. h   7. b

Exercise 5 (p. 113)

2. If I hadn't overslept, I wouldn't have been late.
3. If he'd taken a jacket, he wouldn't have complained all evening about the cold.
4. If Susan had known about the party, she would have gone.
5. If I'd read the newspaper, I would have known what happened yesterday.
6. If they'd had a tent, they would have gone camping.

Exercise 6 (p. 114)

2. a   4. b   6. b   8. b
3. b   5. a   7. a

Exercise 7 (p. 115)

Sample answers:

2. I wish I understood math better./I wish I'd studied harder.
3. I wish I weren't so late./I wish I'd left on time.
4. I wish I could give someone else the check./I wish I hadn't offered to pay the bill.

Exercise 8 (p. 116)

A. 2. If Lee hadn't persuaded Jake to go, he wouldn't have danced with Diane.
   3. If Jake hadn't met Diane, he wouldn't have moved to Texas.

B. 1. If the truck hadn't spilled chemicals, the chemicals wouldn't have polluted the river.
   2. If the truck hadn't crashed into the bridge, the children would have had a place to swim.

C. 1. If there hadn't been a war, my parents wouldn't/ might not have left Honduras.
   2. If my father hadn't had a cousin in Mexico, they wouldn't/couldn't/might not have gone there.
   3. If my dad's cousin hadn't found my father a job in a hotel, my dad wouldn't have bought the hotel.

Exercise 9 (p. 117)

Answers will vary.

See page 155 for Key to Reveiw: Chapters 15-16.

Chapter 17 Noun Clauses

Exercise 1 (p. 121)

1. line 3: that you want to work in marketing
  line 4: what that really means
  line 5: what you want to be later on
  line 9: where you might like to work
  line 10: that you have a certain level of maturity and ambition

line 14: that she wanted to move from computer science into public relations
line 18: that you work hard
line 19: whether or not they should give you more challenging assignments
line 21: how you can become an intern

2. line 3: want   line 14: wanted
  line 4: means   line 19: work
  line 5: want   line 19: should give
  line 9: might like line 21: can become
  line 10: have

Exercise 2 (p. 122)

2. Yuji isn't sure **whether** or not he wants to be a doctor.
3. Do you remember what time **we left**?
4. Do you know **whether** we have to pay or not?
5. I'd like to find out **if/whether** that class **is required**.
6. Have you decided **if/whether** you're coming with **us?**
7. I wonder how **he can** do that.
8. I'm not sure what **I'll** do.
9. Do you have any idea who **she was**?
10. I couldn't have know **whether** it was a winning lottery ticket or not.
11. Could you explain what the theory of relativity **is**?
12. I wonder how many years this program **has been** on TV.

Exercise 3 (p. 123)

Answers will vary. Some examples are:

2. I knew my parents were talking about me, but I couldn't hear **what they were saying.**
3. I'd like to study at Harvard, but it depends on whether **my grades are good enough.**
4. I was going to call you late last night, but I didn't know if **you were still awake.**
5. If you're upset about it, you should tell your friend how **you feel.**
6. We found a package in front of the door yesterday, but we don't know who **sent it.**
7. The bank will give us a loan, but they need to know how much **we need.**
8. I had my umbrella a minute ago. Now I don't remember where **I put it.**
9. It's my grandmother's birthday today, but nobody knows how old **she is.**
10. I'm really hungry, but I can't decide what **I want to eat.**

Exercise 4 (p. 123)

2. Could you tell me **what time/when the plane from Chicago arrives?**
3. I'm trying to find out **where the nearest post office is.**
4. Can you tell me **how much the dinner special is/costs?**
5. I was wondering **if I could move in next week/whether it would be OK to move in next week.**
6. Could you tell me **what your first acting jobs were/how you got started as an actor?**

Exercise 5 (p. 124)

2. a   4. b, c   6. a, b   8. c
3. b   5. c   7. a, b, c

Exercise 6 (p. 125)

2. I thought (that) this was an easy assignment.
3. I believed (that) the class would be easy.
4. I was sure (that) I wouldn't have any problems passing.
5. I knew (that) you liked that movie.
6. I thought (that) you had/you'd seen it already.
7. I assumed (that) you wanted to see it again.
8. I expected (that) you'd/you would go with me.
9. I was sure (that) there wouldn't be any delays at the airport.
10. I thought (that) he didn't eat meat.

Exercise 7 (p. 126)

Sarah: I thought it~~'s~~ _it was_ on the table.

Kim: No, it's not. By the way, do you know ~~that~~ _whether_ the biology assignment is due tomorrow or on Monday?

Sarah: I believe it's due tomorrow.

Kim: Oh no! Nancy said _it's_ ~~is~~ due Monday! I thought I _had_ ~~have~~ the whole weekend. I'd better tell her. Do you know what~~'s~~ her number _is_?

Sarah: I'm afraid not.

Kim: I wonder if _she's_ ~~she~~ at Emily's house. You know, I really don't understand why ~~do~~ we have to do the assignment, anyway. Do you think ⟨is⟩ there going to be a test on it?

B: I don't think so. I hope not! If there is, I'm not sure _if_ ~~what~~ I'm going to pass the class!

Exercise 8 (p. 127)

Answers will vary.

Chapter 18 Reported Speech

Exercise 1 (p. 128)

1. line 14: The woman told police that she had closed her bank account and that she always carried her money with her because she was afraid of burglars.
   line 21: . . . she asked to meet the taxi driver in person.
   line 23: . . . she asked the young man if he wanted a reward . . .
   line 24: he said that he was just doing his job.
   line 25: He then advised the woman to put the money in a bank.

2. line 14: told
   line 21: asked
   line 23: asked
   line 24: said
   line 26: advised

Exercise 2 (p. 129)

1. She asked them **to wait** because **the sheriff might ask them for a statement**.
2. The witness said **he was sure that he had seen a UFO.**
3. The woman said **she didn't believe in UFOs**, but she admitted **that she had never seen anything like it before**.
4. The farmer claimed that **the object had stopped right over his house, and then it had disappeared.**
5. The couple reported that **they had followed it for fifty miles in their car** and said that **they had taken some photos.**
6. A boy asked **what a UFO was.** He also wanted to know **if it was something like a jet.**

Exercise 3 (p. 130)

SHE TOLD	SHE SAID	SHE ASKED	
	✓		2. _____ she'd be on time.
		✓	3. _____ us if we'd be there.
	✓		4. _____ that she was working.
✓			5. _____ us that she'd be late.
✓		✓	6. _____ us to be there at six.
		✓	7. _____ when we'd arrive.
	✓		8. _____ that the meeting should start on time.

Exercise 4 (p. 130)

2. "I ('ve) met you before."
3. "I'm angry at my brother."
4. "I'll help you tomorrow."
5. "You look like your mother."
6. "I'm arriving next Monday."

Exercise 5 (p. 131)

2. The electric company announced that the electricity would be turned off in our area between 10:00 and 11:00 A.M. the next day.
3. Mom reminded Lee that it could get cold in the mountains.
4. Bill admitted that he hadn't had time to finish the report.

5. A man shouted that someone was hurt and that he needed a doctor.
6. The hotel guest complained that the room was dirty and that there weren't any towels.
7. The mechanic promised that he would take a look at my car as soon as possible.
8. The professor pointed out that there were several misspelled words in my paper.

Exercise 6 (p. 132)

2. a, c	4. a, b	6. b, c	8. a, b
3. c	5. a	7. a, c	

Exercise 7 (p. 133)

Answers will vary. Some examples are:

2. if/whether	7. said
3. had	8. said
4. hadn't	9. told/advised
5. 'd/would	10. to
6. told	

Exercise 8 (p. 134)

Answers will vary.

See page 155 for Key to Review: Chapters 17-18.

Key to Chapter Reviews

Review: Chapters 1–3

A.
1. c
2. b
3. c
4. a
5. a
6. c
7. a
8. b
9. b
10. c
11. c
12. b
13. c
14. a

B.
15. How ~~was~~ *did* the fire ~~starting~~ *start*?
16. The children ~~played~~ *were playing* in the yard when it started to rain.
17. The movie is about a group of teenagers who ~~are getting~~ *get* lost in the forest.
18. I know these jeans ~~are looking~~ *look* terrible, but all my other pants are in the laundry.
19. When Kedra was a child, she ~~would have~~ *had* a lot of friends.
20. Marcus and I won't be getting ~~marry~~ *married* next year because we just broke off our engagement.
21. The Chiefs will be the champions this year because they're definitely ~~winning~~ *going to win* tomorrow night's game.
22. I promise that I will ~~be finishing~~ *finish* my homework.
23. If you have time, will you ~~be stopping~~ *stop* and pick up some bread on your way home?
24. Carlos is usually ~~being~~ very level-headed, but today he's overreacting to everything.
25. I was jogging in the park ~~while~~ *when* I fell and hurt my left ankle.

C. 26. b, c 27. b, c 28. a, b 29. b, d 30. a, d

Review: Chapters 4–6

A.
1. How long have the police been trying to solve that crime?
2. How long had the police been trying to solve that crime?
3. X
4. How long did the police try to solve that crime?
5. 2, 4
6. We'd shopped at that store for years.
7. We shopped at the store for years.
8. We've been shopping at that store for years.
9. 6, 7
10. They've had that car since 1998.
11. They'd had that car since 1998.
12. X
13. X
14. X
15. 10

B.
16. e
17. c
18. d
19. g
20. b
21. f
22. a

C.
23. X
Jenny **had** been walking for hours when she noticed it was late.
24. ✓
25. X
Yuji **has** been cooking all day for the party.
26. X
Until we went to France last year, **we'd** never eaten snails.
27. ✓
28. X
Alex won the perfect-attendance award because he **hadn't missed** a day since school started.
29. X
The American Revolutionary War **lasted** from 1775 to 1783.
30. ✓

Review: Chapters 7–8

A.
1. I heard on Channel 7 that we could have a severe storm tonight.
2. You might have grown taller if you had eaten your spinach at every meal.
3. It has got to be very difficult for you to see your friend sick.
4. He should have been here an hour ago.
5. I'm fairly certain this shouldn't take more than about five minutes.
6. That rumor about Rick can't possibly be true!
7. We really ought to call Paulo tonight.
8. She may not be coming to class today.

B.
9. He may need the money./He might need the money./He could need the money.
10. He must be saving for a car./He has to be saving for a car./He's got to be saving for a car.
11. Hiro's boss should be grateful./Hiro's boss ought to be grateful.
12. Hiro must be exhausted./Hiro had to be exhausted./Hiro has got to be exhausted.

13. She could have taken the phone off the hook./
She might have taken the phone off the hook./
She may have taken the phone off the hook.
14. She must have been talking to her boyfriend./
She had to have been talking to her boyfriend./
She has to have been talking to her boyfriend./
She's got to have been talking to her boyfriend.
15. Her phone could be out of order./Her phone
might be out of order./Her phone may be out of
order.
16. She couldn't have been on the phone that long!/
She can't have been on the phone that long!
17. She couldn't be old enough to drive!/She can't
be old enough to drive!
18. She must have had a birthday recently./She
might have had a birthday recently.
19. She should drive carefully.

C. 20. b   26. c
21. a, b, d   27. a, b, c, d
22. b, d   28. d
23. d   29. b, d
24. b, c   30. b, c
25. a, b

Review: Chapters 9–11

A. 1. a   6. c
2. c   7. c
3. a   8. a
4. b   9. a
5. b   10. b

B. 11. to take
12. keeping
13. to play
14. meeting
15. making
16. waiting
17. talking
18. playing

C. 19. Children in the United States are encouraged to
express themselves.
20. The trip will be canceled if the weather is bad.
21. The kingdom of Ethiopia was founded around
1000 B.C.
22. The next book in the series is already being
advertised.
23. Cans and bottles should be recycled.
24. A lot of research has been done in this area.

D. 25. I came to the United States ~~for~~ to study English.

26. Martha's parents wouldn't let her ~~to~~ go out with
her friends.

27. When I saw how much I had upset my sister with
the news, I regretted ~~to tell~~ telling it to her.

28. All students ~~require~~ are required to hand in their
assignments on time.

29. Her father always wants ~~that~~ Lucy to help him
when she wants to be with her friends.

30. The cost of living ~~was~~ increased a lot during the
1970s.

Review: Chapters 12–14

A. 1. b, c
2. b, c
3. b
4. a, b
5. a, b
6. a, c

B. 7. a   14. the
8. a   15. the
9. a   16. the
10. Ø   17. a
11. Ø   18. an
12. the   19. a
13. the

C. 20. I gave the book to a friend of mine who likes science
fiction.

21. What's the name of the restaurant that all the
rock stars go to?

22. One day Dad came home with a large box, ~~that~~ which
he put on the top shelf of the hall closet.

23. That's the same guy who ~~he~~ was working in the
supermarket.

24. Susan wears black boots and a leather jacket
that ~~have~~ has several buttons missing.

25. My neighbor, who had seen the accident, was
interviewed by the police.

D. 26. I wanted to buy a present for a person I like very
much.
27. Last Saturday I went to a mall that/which is near
my home.
28. I was hoping to find a present that/which would
not be too expensive.
29. I had some money I had saved from my part-
time job.
30. When I got on the streetcar, I saw a face I
recognized.

Review: Chapters 15–16

A.
1. a 5. a
2. a 6. b
3. b 7. b
4. b 8. a

B.
9. Will 13. didn't
10. would 14. won't
11. have 15. doesn't
12. Would 16. wouldn't

C.
17. If something isn't done, many people will lose their homes.
18. If I had read the material, I would have been able to follow/could have followed the lecture.
19. If they hadn't practiced a lot, the soccer team wouldn't have won the game.
20. Unless we arrive early, we won't get good seats.
21. If I had studied, my grades wouldn't have been (so) low/ would have been higher.
22. If the workers hadn't complained to the boss, conditions wouldn't have improved.
23. Unless I know someone there, I won't go to a party by myself.
24. If you had listened to my advice, you wouldn't have been sorry.

D.
25. "I'm an only child, and I wish I'm not. [weren't]
26. If I have [had] a brother or a sister, I can [could] hang out with them.
27. Maybe they would introduce me to their friends and I could get to know more people."
28. "I have five brothers and two sisters, so whenever I would need to talk, there is always someone to talk to.
29. One of my brothers or sisters could [can] always help me out.
30. I can't imagine what my life will [would] be like if my parents hadn't decided to have a large family."

Review: Chapters 17–18

A.
1. a 5. b
2. a 6. a
3. b 7. c
4. a 8. c

B.
9. My father asked me what was the reason for my bad grades.
10. My mother thinks what [that] the newspapers tell the truth.
11. I don't know how many students are there [there are] in my class.
12. Some people don't care that [whether] they work or not.
13. The situation is so bad that people don't know when will they [they will] be able to go home.
14. Some people say that that [there] are not enough jobs for students.
15. You have to know what are your priorities.
16. You don't realize how difficult is the work.

C.
17. what time it is
18. if/whether it's time to go
19. if/whether he likes it
20. when it starts
21. where Ben went
22. if/whether they found anything
23. what she did

D.
24. The real estate agent recommended that they look at the house.
25. He reminded them that they wanted a view of the ocean.
26. He admitted that the house needed a little work.
27. He warned them that they would have to decide fast.
28. He mentioned that the house had a garage.
29. He explained that the price was low because the owners wanted to move.
30. He insisted that they go and see it.

Answer Key   155